T0196418

You Are Spirit

An Understanding of Who You Are

Bill Arthur

WESTBOW
PRESS®
A DIVISION OF THOMAS NELSON
& ZONDERVAN

Scripture taken from the New King James Version. Copyright © 1979, 1980, 1982 by Thomas Nelson, Inc. Used by permission. All rights reserved.

WestBow Press books may be ordered through booksellers or by contacting:

WestBow Press
A Division of Thomas Nelson & Zondervan
1663 Liberty Drive
Bloomington, IN 47403
www.westbowpress.com
1 (866) 928-1240

ISBN: 978-1-5127-6676-9 (sc)
ISBN: 978-1-5127-6675-2 (e)

Library of Congress Control Number: 2016919889

Print information available on the last page.

WestBow Press rev. date: 3/13/2017

Contents

Preface

If you're reading this book, you may be searching for something: the answer to the feeling that there is something down deep inside you, the feeling that you're more than what you appear to be.

My prayer is that through this book I will be able to reveal to you what that is.

Science will try to tell you that people have evolved like animals, but if that is true, then why have people been the only living beings in creation that have been able to accomplish what we have? There are many different ideas and philosophies on where people came from and how they developed into what and who they are. This book brings a revelation of the truth of that. It comes from the Word of God, the Bible.

Before I can teach the function of the spiritual realm and the means for walking in the Spirit, I must first reveal who you are in relation to it.

Acknowledgments

God, in His great love, has shown that love for me by putting incredible people in my life. As much as Simon had to help the Lord carry His cross, so too have you all helped me to fulfill the Lord's desire to have this book published.

To my wife, who keeps me uplifted in prayer when the world gets heavy.

To Kirk and Carla for your help and friendship: may God bless you with all your hearts' desires.

To Jim and Melissa, who throughout the years have been such an incredible blessing to me and my family: may God's blessing and favor overtake you and cover you in everything you do, everywhere you go, and with everyone you meet.

To my brothers and sisters in Christ: your prayers and support have touched me greatly, and I love you all.

To the Lord of Hosts and our Father in heaven: You are awesome, and my love and appreciation for You is eternal.

Introduction

The spiritual realm for Christians should be more real than the natural realm we live in. If you are a Christian—one whom God has called to be His spiritual son or daughter through the receiving of His Son, Jesus, for the forgiveness of sins—you have become alive spiritually, your name being written in the Lamb's Book of Life.

You see, as Jesus told Nicodemus, you must be born again. Everyone is born physically alive and spiritually dead, and by being born again (which I will go over later), you became alive spiritually by the power of the Holy Spirit. By putting your thoughts and desires aside, and by being led by the Spirit of God, you bring this scripture to pass: "I have been crucified with Christ; it is no longer I who live, but Christ lives in me; and the *life* which I now live in the flesh I live by faith in the Son of God, who loved me and gave Himself for me." (Galatians 2:20).

This book is written to teach you that you can walk and live in the Spirit of God—and to reveal the truth about who and what you are.

You Are Spirit

In the Beginning

If we start off in the beginning of the Bible, the book of Genesis, we can read about how God created everything. In this book I'm only concerned with people—where people came from, how they are made, and what they are made of. After God created the earth, sun, moon, and stars, He created the fish and the animals. And then, as recorded in Genesis 1:26, He created man.

Then God said, "Let Us make man in Our image, according to Our likeness; let them have dominion over the fish of the sea, over the birds of the air, and over the cattle, over all the earth and over every creeping thing that creeps on the earth." So God created man in His *own* image; in the image of God He created him; male and female He created them. Then God blessed them, and God said to them, "Be fruitful and multiply; fill the earth and subdue it; have dominion over the fish of the sea, over the birds of the air, and over every living thing that moves on the earth." (Genesis 1:26–28).

I want to point out that in this passage of scripture God spoke in a way that shows He was speaking to someone else. He used the words "make man in *our* image and after *our* likeness." So then we have to ask ourselves, "Who was God speaking to?" In the New Testament in the book of John, chapter 1, God explained how this all came about. "In the beginning was the Word, and the Word was with God, and the Word was God. He was in the beginning with God. All things were made through Him, and without Him nothing was made that was made. In Him was life, and the life was the light of men." (John 1:1–4) It says here that all things were made by Him and for Him, and this is talking about God's Word. We were created by the Word of God. This passage says that all things were made by Him and for Him, and without Him was nothing made. Hebrews 11:3 talks about faith. It says, "By faith we understand that the worlds were framed by the word of God, so that the things which are seen were not made of things which are visible."

Faith is the spiritual substance that, when mixed with the word of God and the power of God, manifests in the natural realm as things that appear. That is how man was created on the earth. God spoke His word. He spoke man into existence in the spiritual realm, and His words mixed with faith manifested man in the natural realm. People are a mixture of spirit (who they really are) and a body (where the spirit resides), and they have a soul, which houses the mind, will, and emotions.

Spiritual Becomes Natural

John 1:14 says, "And the Word became flesh and dwelt among us, and we beheld His glory, the glory as of the only begotten of the Father, full of grace and truth." To try to grasp an understanding of what this says, picture the words that you speak, and put them into a body that looks exactly like you. That is where the words that you speak take on a body that looks just like you. Can you see your words when you speak them? Of course not. So what are they? Your words are an expression of yourself, your thoughts, your feelings, and your attitudes. Since they are invisible, they are spiritual in nature. They do not have a physical existence, but they do exist. If you were to put them into a body and give that body life, then you would be doing exactly what God did to create man.

Genesis 1:27 states "So God created man in His *own* image; in the image of God He created him; male and female He created them." Where did God create them? Genesis 2:7 says, "And the LORD God formed man *of* the dust of the ground, and breathed into his nostrils the breath of life; and man became a living being. If man wasn't formed until Genesis 2:7, where was man when God created him in Genesis 1:27? The Bible says that God created man in His image and likeness, and before we can understand this, we need to get an understanding of God. In John 4:24 God told us, "God *is* Spirit, and those who worship Him must worship in spirit and truth." Since this scripture proclaims that God is a spirit, we can conclude that, being made in His image and His likeness, we are spirit as well. Back in Genesis, God said, "Let us make man in our image and likeness." Because His words are spirit, they created spiritual men and women. As it says in John 1:14, the Word became flesh, and that is exactly what happened when God created man. He created spiritual man in Genesis 1 and then made him a natural body in chapter 2. And then He breathed His spirit into the body, and man became a living soul.

The Image and Likeness of God

The word of God says that man is created in His image and likeness. If this is true, and man has a body, a soul, and a spirit, then must God also have a body, a soul, and a spirit? The soul consists of the mind, the will, and the emotions. In order for God to speak a concept, He must have a mind to develop that concept. Throughout scripture God reveals the things that please Him and the things that displease Him, which shows that He has emotions and a soul. As we have already seen, God declared that He is spirit. We have seen that man and woman were created with a body, and they became living souls. In this we see that man is exactly in the image and likeness of God as far as creation goes. From here we need to get an understanding of what it means to be a spirit. Through our lives we know and understand thoughts, feelings, and desires. We also understand our bodies and how they operate and function with nerves, cardiovascular system, muscles, and so on. But very little is taught or understood about the spiritual side of man.

Spiritual Kingdoms

In order for us to get an understanding of functioning in the realm of the spirit, we must understand that there are two different realms of the spirit. There is the realm of *righteousness*. That is the kingdom of God. God's kingdom has a king, and His name is Jesus Christ. The other kingdom is a kingdom of *darkness*. There is a ruler over that darkness. His name is Lucifer, or Satan. These two kingdoms are at war with each other, and the prize they are fighting for is the soul of man. Whichever kingdom you subject yourself to, that is the kingdom that will rule over your life. When you allow God to rule your spirit, body, and soul, you have His promise of blessings. Those blessings will continue forever when the spiritual and natural realms combine for all of eternity.

The kingdom of darkness has already been judged by God, and at the appointed time it will be destroyed. Satan and all the souls of men he has managed to capture through deception, seduction, or lies will be destroyed as well. For the sake of this book, we are only going to focus on how to function in the earth as the spirit person that God created you to be—and how to function in His kingdom.

The book of Genesis 1:28 says that God gave man dominion—dominance—over the earth and everything in it. 1:28 Then God blessed them, and God said to them, "Be fruitful and multiply; fill the earth and *subdue it*; have *dominion* over the fish of the sea, over the birds of the air, and over every living thing that moves on the earth." And it goes further in Luke 10:19 "Behold, I give you the authority to trample on serpents and scorpions, and over all the power of the enemy, and nothing shall by any means hurt you." Those who understand and believe who they are by these verses allow God to function through them and will manifest, or prove, their dominance over the world and everything in it, and also over the kingdom of darkness by the power of God. The Holy Spirit and God's angels will manifest in and through them because of their faith.

The people who have the kingdom of darkness operating spiritually through them are also in the world. These are people who propagate evil, darkness, and death because they have areas of themselves that the kingdom of darkness controls through sin. The people in the kingdom of darkness have some dominance in the earth. The people that have the spirits of darkness (demonic angels or demons) do have some power but it fails in comparison to the power of God.

As a person you are a tube, or vessel, through which the spiritual realm flows, either for righteousness or evil. Each kingdom has spirits or beings that can manifest in the natural realm and can have an influence on and *through* man. God has angels, and the devil has demons. These beings will enter and manifest through God's creation. In the Bible there are many instances of animals speaking and inanimate objects doing the impossible—like water flowing from a rock or an iron ax-head swimming. The spirits also enter into people if they have the ability to. The well-known movie from the 1970s, the *Exorcist*, was a showdown between the power of God in priests and the power of Satan in a little girl. The movie was based on a true story, but it was actually a little boy who had become possessed. The power of God in the priests made the demon of the kingdom of darkness leave proving which kingdom has the greater power.

When God moved upon my heart and drew me close to Him, I held up the Bible and told God to reveal to me the truth. I said that either the world was true and nothing in the Bible could change the world, or the Bible was true and I could change the world by what was in the Bible. As I began to read the Bible and see what it said about who I was as God's child, and being one with His spirit, I began to learn how to function in that capacity. I began to exercise dominion over the things of this earth.

Ephesians 1:18–23 explains how Jesus was resurrected and placed as the head and ruler with all authority, both naturally and spiritually, over the kingdom of God, the kingdom of darkness, and everything that is named and how he has extended that power unto us. " the eyes of your understanding being enlightened; that you may know what is the hope of His calling, what are the riches of the glory of His inheritance in the saints, and what *is* the exceeding greatness of His power toward us who believe, according to the working of His mighty power which He worked in Christ when He raised Him from the dead and seated *Him* at His right hand in the heavenly *places,* far above all principality and power and might and dominion, and every name that is named, not only in this age but also in that which is to come. And He put all *things* under His feet, and gave Him *to be* head over all *things* to the church, which is His body, the fullness of Him who fills all in all." Can you think of anything that does not have a name? No, everything has a name, whether you know what that name is or not. Ephesians 2:6 says, "and raised *us* up together, and made *us* sit together in the heavenly *places* in Christ Jesus." So, spiritually, through Jesus Christ and the Holy Spirit, we have the spiritual power and authority to exercise God's will on earth, just as Jesus did and the sitting is talking about sitting in the same seat of power and authority.

Becoming Godly

There seems to be somewhat of a disconnect between what the Bible says and what people actually believe. The Bible says in 1 John 4:17, "Love has been perfected among us in this: that we may have boldness in the day of judgment; because *as he is, so are we in this world.*" Many people have a hard time accepting this or even believing it, because they see the perfection of Jesus Christ and the imperfection of themselves. But in order to believe this scripture, you also have to take other scriptures in context with it.

Romans 4:17 says, "(as it is written, "I have made you a father of many nations") in the presence of Him whom he believed—God, who gives life to the dead and calls those things which *do not exist as though they did*;" Does this mean that God is lying to Himself? God forbid. God is applying His own faith to His desire for us to be just like Him, and He is speaking that forth to make it come to pass. Isaiah 46:10 says, "Declaring the end from the beginning, And from ancient times *things* that are not *yet* done, Saying, 'My counsel shall stand, And I will do all My pleasure." So, when people look at themselves now, they see themselves either in the beginning stage or somewhere along the path toward the end where they become what God has said. If people believe what God has said, they can be what God has said *now.* This is God's desire.

Romans 8:19 says, " For the earnest expectation of the creation eagerly waits for the revealing of the sons of God." If the Father is spirit, then the sons must also be spirit and function spiritually. In the Gospel of John, chapter 3, Jesus was speaking with Nicodemus and telling him that he must be born again. Nicodemus, using his worldly mind and his own understanding, did not understand the realm of the spirit. He asked, "Is it possible to go back into the mother's womb?" Jesus answered him, saying that unless one is born of *water* and of *spirit*, he cannot see the kingdom of God. He went on to say, "That which is born of the flesh is flesh, and that which is born of the Spirit is spirit." Hebrews 12:9 states, "Furthermore, we have had human fathers who corrected *us,* and we paid *them* respect. Shall we not much more readily be in subjection to the Father of spirits and live?" The only way we can grasp an understanding of our being like Jesus is to understand and accept that we are not just born of flesh but that we can be born again of spirit. This is not something that people can do themselves. It is something only God can accomplish, and it is done only through faith.

God chooses those whom He will have in His family. God offers the sacrifice of His Son Jesus to all, but scripture says, "For many are called, but few *are* chosen." (Matthew 22:14). When we are called by God, and we accept that calling, God gives us the power to be His son or daughter by believing in Jesus Christ (who died for our sins), believing that God is the Father of Him, and accepting Jesus's death as the payment for the punishment for our sins against the Father. When sin is removed, then we are the recipients of God's righteousness. After removing our sin through Jesus Christ's sacrifice for us, He puts the Holy Spirit in us and gives us His righteousness. Then we have the right and legal authority to operate within His power, presence, and kingdom. It states in the book of Isaiah 54:17 "No weapon formed against you shall prosper, And every tongue *which* rises against you in judgment You shall condemn. This *is* the heritage of the servants of the LORD, And their righteousness *is* from Me," Says the LORD. It is because you are righteous in the eyes of God by being born again, that no weapon formed against you will prosper and now we have the right and legal authority to operate in the spiritual realm to perform God's will and manifest the power of God. We cannot be righteous on our own. It is only through the power of the Holy Spirit—and our submitting to Him, His will, and His desires—that we can walk as Jesus walked on this earth.

He has also given us the ability to work with the angels. Hebrews 1:14 says that "Are they not all ministering spirits sent forth to minister for those who will inherit salvation?" — meaning, those who have accepted Jesus as their savior and the Father as their God have the angels sent to accomplish the things that *we say* to bring glory to God through us. We have the legal right to use His power to glorify Him and to pursue the very reason He gave us His power: to destroy the work of Satan and his kingdom of darkness. "He who sins is of the devil, for the devil has sinned from the beginning. For this purpose the Son of God was manifested, that He might destroy the works of the devil." (1 John 3:8). As a son/daughter of God, that has become our job as well. This is the reason God has given us authority over the Enemy by seating us with Christ at the right hand of the Father far above, in authority and power over all the power that the Enemy has in his kingdom. And we are to be going forth, destroying the Enemy's works and proclaiming the kingdom of God. That is why the scripture says that the gates of hell shall not prevail against the church (Mathew 16:18). It's because we have more power and a higher authority. The Enemy is not supposed to be coming against our gates or the kingdom of righteousness; we are supposed to be tearing his gates down. We are supposed to be on the offense, not the defense. God has given us spiritual armor and a spiritual sword to fight spirits with. The Enemy has done an outstanding job of getting Christians to put down the Sword of the Spirit and not war against his kingdom because of fear and not knowing the power and authority God has given us. Picture a world where there is no police force or government authority, and people just do whatever they want. If the people's desire was to do evil against others, and there was no police force, evil would prevail, because there would be nothing stopping it. Without Christians walking as Christ, full of the Holy Spirit, that is exactly what this world would be. God's kingdom runs on rules and laws that are governed by righteousness. As Christians we are to enforce God's laws against the lawlessness of Satan and his kingdom by using the power and authority given to us by our faith in Jesus Christ and our receiving of the Holy Spirit. The scripture Ephesians 6:12 says "For we do not wrestle against flesh and blood, but against principalities, against powers, against the rulers of the darkness of this age, against spiritual *hosts* of wickedness in the heavenly *places*." We don't fight against the person who is doing evil; we battle spiritually against the spiritual power that is in them and causing them to do evil. That is why the scripture says we do not wrestle against flesh and blood but against powers and principalities and spiritual wickedness in high places. The Enemy's spirits are just controlling the people. God doesn't control us; He wants us to *let* Him have control.

In 1 Samuel 10:6, the scripture says "Then the Spirit of the LORD will come upon you, and you will prophesy with them and be turned into another man." When the Spirit of God comes on you, you don't stay a worldly, natural man. Instead you become a new man, a spiritual man; and the old man—the carnal, worldly man—passes away. In Mark 2:21,22 Jesus said "No one sews a piece of unshrunk cloth on an old garment; or else the new piece pulls away from the old, and the tear is made worse. And no one puts new wine into old wineskins; or else the new wine bursts the wineskins, the wine is spilled, and the wineskins are ruined. But new wine must be put into new wineskins." The new wine is the Holy Spirit. The Holy Spirit is not placed into the old, carnal, worldly man. It is placed into the new man, the spiritual man, the man of God.

From here we must learn what and who that new man is so that we do not continue to act like the old man.

The Beginning of Understanding

Before we can accept having a spiritual life as Christians, we have to get a lot of understanding and revelation about the spiritual realm. How can you participate in something that you do not know or understand?

The Lord told me that I have to brainwash people. That is, I need to wash from people's minds their worldly ways of thinking, worldly wisdom, and all the things they've learned from the world that are against God. We have to use the word of God—through the power of the Holy Spirit—to wash out all the lies that have formed our opinions and thought patterns based on the lies of this world, which our life experiences tell us are the truth. We continually need to have the world and its ways washed out of our minds in order to go to a deeper spiritual understanding and revelation of God. It's like putting a new operating system in your computer and getting rid of the old one. Romans 12:2 says "and do not be conformed to this world, but be transformed by the renewing of your mind, that you may prove what *is* that good and acceptable and perfect will of God." In order to transform into the spiritual person you are, you have to transform your mind from what the world tells you is real. Being an earthly human person, you must learn to be the spiritual person that God created you to be. All the things you have learned that are against God and scripture, things the world has lied to you about, must be replaced by the truth of God's word.

When I was a kid, my mom always made broccoli, and she left the stems on it. My mother always called it "trees," because that was what it looked like. When I was in fifth grade I had a health and nutrition class, and there was a page in the book with a bunch of vegetables on it. The teacher was calling on students to tell what vegetables were there. It was the only time I'd ever raised my hand, and the teacher called on me. I said, "Those are trees," and everybody started laughing. The teacher said, "No," and I said, "Yes, those are trees!" because that was what I had been taught. The teacher proceeded to tell me that it was broccoli. So I went home mad and upset at my mother for teaching me that broccoli was *trees*.

As you can see, we learn many things that are not true. Lots of ideas about the spiritual realm are not taught from God's word. They come from books and movies and other means that are not the truth. You get a lot of untruth from Hollywood and from churches that haven't really studied the spiritual realm. They just throw ideas and imagination out there that have no revelation of the truth. Many people are led to believe a host of lies and made-up claims about the spiritual realm, which are passed off as being the truth. Since the spiritual realm interacts with the natural realm quite often, we hear of ghost stories and stories of angels and God's intervention in people's lives, but that does not give us an understanding of how we function in the spiritual realm. Most people believe the spiritual realm is real and exists. Some people do not. So we must start by gaining an understanding of what is real.

What Is Real?

What is the definition of the word *real*? The definition of *real* is "something that has existence or actuality as a thing representing truth." The devil and the world try to make you think that a lot of things in this world are real when they are not. Though they may be perceived as real and true, they are not. A magician uses an illusion to convince people to believe that something really happened, but the truth is that it is just an illusion. When the truth is revealed about the illusion, we then understand that it was just a trick and not real. The same is true when we compare the illusion of the world's perceived reality to the truth of God's word.

Many children have probably had the old "I've got your nose" trick played on them. An adult grabs the child's nose and then displays his thumb sticking out between his fingers. He makes the child believe that he really has gotten the child's nose by showing the child something that looks true. The child's perception is that he sees his nose in the adult's hand. That game has probably caused more childhood trauma to innocent emotions than anything else, and that is exactly what the devil wants to do to us. He wants to get us to act and think emotionally instead of spiritually in truth.

The word *true* means "faithful to fact or reality." So, now we have to determine what fact and reality are. Either God's word is fact and reality, or the world is fact and reality, because they contradict each other. So you're going to believe one and come against the other, because you can't believe them both.

In 1 Kings 18:21 Elijah was on the mountain with all the people and prophets of Baal. He said, "And Elijah came to all the people, and said, "How long will you falter between two opinions? If the LORD *is* God, follow Him; but if Baal, follow him." What Elijah said is basically the same situation we have today. If God is real and His word is true, then believe what His word says, regardless of what you see portrayed by the facade of the world.

Faith

Most Christians have heard this before: "Faith is the *substance* of things hoped for and the evidence of things not seen" (Hebrews 11:1). In the spiritual realm there is a substance that is used to transform spiritual stuff into natural stuff. It's called faith. *Faith* means "confidence in or dependence on."

Every one of us has been given a measure of faith (Romans 12:3). We are responsible for what we do with that faith. We can apply our faith to God's word, and our faith—mixed with God's word and the power of that word—will manifest what the word says in the natural realm. The Enemy knows and wants to stop this, so he will put all sorts of pressure on us to not believe what God says in order to make us feel hopeless and helpless. He wants us to believe that there is absolutely nothing we can do.

Proverbs 23:7 says "For as he thinks in his heart, so *is* he." What a person believes is what he will act out and react to. Have you ever seen beautiful people who think they are ugly? Maybe this is because when they were younger they were told all the time that they were ugly, and over the years they began to believe it. Since that is what they believe, that is how they are going to feel and act. The truth is that they are beautiful, but they have believed a lie.

The devil works overtime to get you not to believe God and not to put your faith in God's word. The devil will tell you things about sins you've committed. He does this to bring in guilt and to make you think that God is mad at you and won't help you because of your sins. If you apply your faith to that lie, you will not have any faith and confidence that God is helping you, and you may become depressed and defeated. We see it all the time: people get defeated by believing lies. They end up making mistakes and going down in defeat and despair. Why not take the faith that we have and apply it to God's word, which says, "In all these things we are more than conquerors" (Romans 8:37)? What if we just believed Romans 8:31: "What then shall we say to these things? If God *is* for us, who *can be* against us?" If a thousand shall fall at my left hand and ten thousand at my right, I shall only be a witness (Psalms 91:7). God doesn't say that trouble and persecution won't come. He says that when it does and your faith is tried, you'll be delivered out of it if you are faithful.

Faith takes the imagination and turns it into a physical or mental reality. If you break down molecules and atoms to the smallest particles that make it up, electrons, protons, and neutrons are what it is made of, you will find faith. Faith takes those particles and arranges them into what the imagination has hoped to create, which fits the scripture Hebrews 11:1 Now faith is the substance of things hoped (imagined) for, the evidence of things not seen. of things *hoped* (imagined) and the evidence of the things that are not seen naturally (but exist spiritually). Do imagined things exist? Sure they do, even if they only exist in the imagination. Take a table, for example. If we break down the atoms that make up the table to their lowest parts and reconfigure them into a different design, we could make up anything that we imagine, because everything is made up of the same atoms, electrons, protons, and neutrons.

So, now we have to understand how to function in decision-making with our will. Your soul is your mind, your will, and your emotions. The devil tries to come against your willpower in order to get you to make bad choices. Your will is the power of conscious, deliberate action by which the mind makes choices and acts to carry them out. Most spiritual interaction isn't out there on the streets or in the schools; it's in your mind, your soul, and your will. That is where the lies of the enemy fight against the truth of God's word to try to get you not to believe what God says. That's why the Bible says, "And let us not grow weary while doing good, for in due season we shall reap if we do not lose heart." (Galatians 6:9). Fighting the lies that come against God's word is spiritual warfare, and doing what is right according to God's word is what the enemy is trying to stop. When you are doing that which is right for God, "He gives power to the weak, And to *those who have* no might He increases strength. Even the youths shall faint and be weary, And the young men shall utterly fall, But those who wait on the LORD shall renew *their* strength; They shall mount up with wings like eagles, They shall run and not be weary, They shall walk and not faint." (Isaiah 40:29–31). When you start feeling weary, do you come into agreement with the weariness that tries to make you say "I can't do this; I'm just too tired"? Or do you go into prayer and hit your knees, saying, "Lord, your word declares that You will renew my strength as the eagles' wings, and I need Your strength right now." Seek Him and enter into His kingdom so that He may renew your strength. We must also walk in wisdom. If we need rest, we need to take it. God gave us the Sabbath (the day of rest), because He knew we needed rest. Even God rested on the seventh day. So there is a trying of our faith in what God says, just as it was for Abraham. God already knows our hearts and everything that we will do. He allows us to be tested so that *we* can know what is in our own hearts—what we truly believe and how we will act. God told Abraham to take his only son up to the mountain and sacrifice him. It was a trial of Abraham's faith. Abraham loved his son, Isaac, and God had promised him that Isaac and his descendants would have a covenant contract with God. Abraham knew that even if he sacrificed Isaac, God would have to raise him up to fulfill His promise. Since Abraham trusted God to fulfill His word to him, Abraham went to sacrifice Isaac, God stopped him and supplied him with a ram to sacrifice. God works with us in the same manner. I'm not saying that we are to go and sacrifice our children, but God will test us to see if we have anything in our hearts that means more to us than He means to us or anything that we believe more than Him. God is a jealous God, and He wants us to put Him first. It is foolish not to. He loves us more than we can understand. God supplies us with all that we need. If a miracle is needed, who besides God can perform it? We need to trust Him, rely on Him, and have faith in Him.

Power

We need to get a revelation about the power of God so we can understand His power; what it's for and how to use it. Scripture says that "For the message of the cross is foolishness to those who are perishing, but to us who are being saved it is the power of God. (1Cor.1:18). *Power* means "strength or force actually put forth; the right, ability, or capacity to exercise control and legal authority." It's the cross of Christ that gives us the legal authority to exercise God's word and its power according to His will. Police officers have the authority of their state to execute power through weapons to enforce the law. God grants us weapons and spiritual power to enforce His will. When you come against demonic spirits, storms, and things such as poverty, sickness, disease, defeat, despair, and despondency, you don't come against them in your own power or authority. You coming against them as one who has received the sacrifice of God and has been cleansed from all unrighteousness. The book of Isaiah says in the later part of Isaiah 54:17, "And their righteousness *is* from Me, Says the Lord." You come at these evil things, as it says in Ephesians 2:6, that God "raised *us* up together, and made *us* sit together in the heavenly *places* in Christ Jesus". So your level of authority is the highest level of authority there is: the authority found at the right hand of the Father. It is from there that you exercise your power and authority through Christ, the Holy Spirit, and the word of God. It is the sacrifice of Jesus on the cross for your sins—and your faith in Him—that gives you the right to do so.

We had a storm coming right toward our city and neighborhood. There were tornados in the storm, and my wife was getting the kids into the laundry room, since there are no windows there. The more I thought about the storm and the damage it could create, the madder I got. So I went outside, looked up at the storm, and stretched forth my hand. Now, you have to remember that the Bible tells us that "You will also declare a thing, And it will be established for you; So light will shine on your ways." (Job 22:28), so I spoke to that storm! I said, "You shall *not* come near my dwelling. No plague, no calamity, no destruction shall come near my house!", which is what God says in Psalm 91:10 "No evil shall befall you, Nor shall any plague come near your dwelling;" As I prayed, an angel appeared at the upper left side of my view of the sky. When I spoke against the storm, the angel took off in the direction of the storm. I did not know what the angel was going to do, but I knew he was there to act upon my words. I brought my family out of the laundry room and sat them in front of the television. We all watched the storm, which was coming right at us, split in two. Half of it went to the north of us, and the other half went to the south of us. It did not come near us! I believe that angel went and cut that storm in half.

In Hebrews 1:14 the Bible tells us, "Are they not all ministering spirits sent forth to minister for those who will inherit salvation?", and in Hebrews 1:7 "Who makes His angels spirits And His ministers a flame of fire." When we do spiritual warfare or exercise godly power and authority, the angels of God are operating through the word of God, bringing what you say to pass. That's why Matthew 18:18 says, "Assuredly, I say to you, whatever you bind on earth will be bound in heaven, and whatever you loose on earth will be loosed in heaven." You're not actually going and grabbing a demon and tying him up, but the angels are. So how do you know that the angels are ministering for you if you can't see what's happening in the invisible spiritual world?

By Faith! It's All by Faith

It's faith in the power of God's word. It's faith in the power of the cross of Calvary to separate you from sin, and faith that makes you righteous unto God, and seats you in the third heaven at the right hand of the Father to give you the power and authority to use God's word. The scripture says, "As Christ is, so are we in this world" (1 John 4:17). Ephesians 2 tells us that Christ is risen and is seated at the right hand of the Father, and we are risen with Him and seated also at the right hand of the Father in Christ.

The story is told in Acts 19:13–16 about some exorcists and the sons of Sceva, who went out and tried to cast a demon out of a man. The account shows the difference between a true believer and a bunch of religious people who don't have faith. "Then some of the itinerant Jewish exorcists took it upon themselves to call the name of the Lord Jesus over those who had evil spirits, saying, "We exorcise you by the Jesus whom Paul preaches." Also there were seven sons of Sceva, a Jewish chief priest, who did so. And the evil spirit answered and said, "Jesus I know, and Paul I know; but who are you?" Then the man in whom the evil spirit was leaped on them, overpowered them, and prevailed against them, so that they fled out of that house naked and wounded. One of the things that the Lord has shared with me is that we can walk the same path that another person has walked yet never meet that person. There are lots of people who follow Christ but have never met Him. Until you have a one-on-one relationship with Jesus Christ, you do not need to be doing anything spiritual, because you may just get beaten and bloodied, and run naked for your life, just like the religious bunch did. You might even get yourself possessed like the Gadarene demoniac.

Not that I want to scare you, but the *Exorcist* movie is based on a true story of a little boy playing with a Ouija board. Spiritual interactions outside of God's word are strictly forbidden by God, because He knows what they will do to us. I have ministered to many who were into witchcraft and the occult. Because of their sin of interactions with that stuff, they suffered mental confusion and destruction, which are almost always the result of getting involved in demonic activity outside of the Bible and God's word.

Before doing anything spiritual, you must get into a right relationship with God through Jesus Christ. You have to be separated, holy unto Him. You need to be cleansed of the things of the world by cleansing your mind and replacing worldly thoughts and beliefs with godly ones, much like removing an old program from a computer and downloading a new way of thinking and believing. You are not going to be perfect. The Bible tells us that until Jesus comes—and we are changed in the twinkling of an eye, and our corruption puts on incorruption (we trade this earthly body for a heavenly body) we will be at war with ourselves. Our new spiritual nature will war against our old worldly nature and its desires. At the same time, you can't walk around full of sin, because sin defiles the conscience, bringing in doubt and unbelief. If your conscience is defiled, it will be hard for you to have faith in God, because you have a separation in that area. Not that God has separated Himself from us, but a defiled conscience will separate us from Him.

To Believe

The scripture says in Proverbs 23:7, "For as he thinks in his heart, so *is* he." To think in your heart is to believe. *Believe* means "to accept as true or real." The problem is that we've been taught so much by worldly knowledge and through circumstances and poor church doctrine that we believe falsehoods. We put our faith in the false, and we make it come to pass. We have to go back to scripture, which talks about "that He (God) might sanctify and cleanse her (the church) with the washing of water by the word."(Ephesians 5:26) That's where we need to be brainwashed. We have to wash out all that nonsense and get back to the word of truth.

The word *belief* means "the acceptance of the truth or actuality of anything without certain proof or confidence." The Bible says, "Cast not away your confidence which has great recompense of reward." You can't be confident in God's love and supply when you're all burdened with sin. Sin causes you to be filled with guilt, shame, and condemnation. God's word doesn't condemn you, but the Holy Spirit brings conviction when there is something about you that is not right and he wants you to change it. His whole desire is for you to be cleansed and holy. The Enemy brings in condemnation with thoughts like, *You're just a dirty rotten sinner, and God's not going to do anything for you*. If you start to believe that, you will feel guilty, and since you feel that way, it becomes the truth to you. Then you will not have any faith that God has separated you from sin, so you believe that you can't receive from Him.

When you separate yourself from sin, your faith level goes up, your confidence goes up, and your holiness and righteousness go up—and you walk with God.

Since you're right with God through the power of the cross by the blood of Jesus washing you clean of sin, you now have faith and confidence in God's word, and there is no separation between you and God even when the devil and things of the world try to come against you. Then you can exercise your power and authority over whatever is coming against you and defeat it. The devil tries hard to get you to believe his lies so that you will be and do what *he* says and not what God says. It's all in what you believe to be true.

The Spirit

The first five books of the Old Testament in the word of God are called the Law. The New Testament says we are not under the law but under the Spirit. During Jesus's life on earth, the Jews had made laws that everyone had to live by. If the Holy Spirit told someone to do something that was against these man-made laws, the religious leaders would say, "What you're doing is illegal." For instance, they had a law that people had to wash their hands before eating. They would say, "You're eating with unwashed hands." But what would happen if the Holy Spirit told someone to eat with dirty hands? Should that person walk in disobedience to the Spirit and wash to fulfill the man-made law?

Most churches teach that in the Old Testament people gave a tenth of everything they earned. The book of Malachi instructed that people bring a tithe (a tenth of what their increase was). This reference to tithing is taken out of context. If you intend to tithe the way most churches say you should, but the Holy Spirit tells you not to give, are you led by the Spirit or by the law of church doctrine?

This is how the Lord broke me of that. Sometimes I was at church, and the Holy Spirit told me not to give. But then there were times when I would go to church, and He'd tell me to give so far above a tenth (tithe) that it was more like 60 to 80 percent. Sometimes He's told me to give everything. The religious say a tenth of your money is God's, but the truth is that it's all God's, all 100 percent of it. If God doesn't want you to give it, it's His. Let Him do with it as He wants. You should not be bound up in the religious doctrine or rules; you have to be led of the Spirit. To be led by the Holy Spirit is to be humble before Him and obedient to do or say whatever He leads you to do or say. In the worldly sense, it may be strange or may even appear not to make any sense at all to do what He says, but if He is God, then who are we to argue?

In America we do not have a king as our government, so it is hard to understand that type of system. All people have flaws, and many kings throughout history have been tyrants to their people. God is not a tyrant, nor is He flawed, so we can have faith that He loves us and wants the best for us. We can trust Him, because He does not lie, break promises, or deceive.

The Enemy, the devil, will try to get you to break God's laws so that he might get God to execute His judgment upon you for being a lawbreaker. If you do not break laws, and you do what is right, then you won't get in trouble. But if you break laws, then you are judged and punished. The Old Testament is full of judgments that are pronounced for the breaking of God's laws. If the devil can get you to break those laws, he goes to God and reminds God of His word of judgment. The name *Satan* actually means "the adversary" or "the accuser of the brethren." If you are led by the Spirit of God, then the Father answers the devil and tells him of your obedience to His spirit, which will not lead you to do anything that is contrary to His law. We also have a lawyer of our own: The Lord Jesus Christ. The grace that comes from Him keeps us from receiving the punishment for our sins, because He took our punishment upon Himself when He was beaten and crucified, and He wants the same spirit that was in Him to be in you.

Getting God in You

God reveals that the Holy Spirit comes and resides within you. "He who is in you" (1 John 4:4). How does the Holy Spirit get into you? When God gets you to a place where you are convicted of your sin, and He leads you to want to be freed from it, you should do as people did in Jesus's time. People came from all over to John the Baptist to confess their sins and be baptized. Baptism is the process of being submerged under water, which signifies being buried in the ground, and then being brought up out of the water, which signifies being resurrected from the ground and raised into new life and your sins and the old sinful you, stays in the water.

There is a problem in many churches because they do not follow this process correctly. The person doing the baptizing asks if the person being baptized has accepted Jesus as his Lord, but there needs to be confession of sin. When people come out of the water, all they are is wet. People are supposed to confess their sins, and then when they are baptized, the sins stay in the water, and the people come out free of sin. This is John's baptism (Acts 19:3–4).

There is another baptism that comes after the water baptism, which many people never go through, and that is the baptism of the Spirit. John the Baptist said that the one who was to come after him would baptize with the Holy Spirit and fire (Matthew 3:11; Luke 3:16; Mark 1:8) John the Baptist explained that it was Jesus Himself who would baptize the people with the Holy Spirit. Baptism is the submerging of your life into the Holy Spirit, much like being submerged in the water. The Holy Spirit is supposed to be in you, on you, and through you so that He lives through your life. The Holy Spirit will then reveal the scriptures to you so that you have the proper understanding of what the scriptures say. Jesus was the Word of God made flesh, and He was baptized in the Holy Spirit (Luke 3:22; Matthew 3:16), so He was word and spirit. When we read the word of God and have the Holy Spirit, we become word and spirit. God told Ezekiel, "Take this scroll and eat it!" (Ezekiel 3:3). What happens when you eat something? Your body breaks it down and uses it, and it becomes a part of you. The same thing happens with the word of God. The more of the word of God you put in you, the more the word of God you become, and the more the word of God comes out of you. This is a spiritual principle that works the same with the things of the world. The more of the things of the world you put in you, the more the world comes out of you.

Watch Out for the World, Be Led of the Spirit

One of the things I had to repent of was watching the news: politics, taxes, death and destruction, and all the worldly stuff going on. All of this stuff was coming through my eyes and into my heart, and it brought with it a bad attitude and darkness. The Bible says in Mathew 6:23, "But if your eye is bad, your whole body will be full of darkness. If therefore the light that is in you is darkness, how great *is* that darkness! In scripture you never see Jesus screaming that Caesar is in control. You do not see Him siding with the Zealots, rioting and saying, "Let's take up arms and kill the Romans." Instead Jesus said, "I must be about my Father's business!" One of the traps of the Enemy is to get us bound up and involved in what's going on in the world. If we go back and look at Jesus's time, we see that the road going to Jerusalem was lined with people who were crucified. There was death and destruction everywhere. The Bible says that Pontius Pilate was the most ruthless ruler ever to govern that area. But do we see Jesus going through and resurrecting everybody off the crosses? Do we see Him going through and solving all the poverty and Roman oppression? Do we see Him going through and healing all who were sick? When He went to the pool of Bethsaida, how many people did He heal? One! How many were there? Bunches! If the Father had wanted Jesus to heal them all, He would have, but He was only doing what the Father was instructing Him to do through the Holy Spirit.

One of the tricks of the Enemy involves spiritual warfare. It comes when you get into scripture and start to understand and recognize the demonic spirits. When you start to see the fruits of those spirits, your natural desire is to go after those spirits and attack them. The Enemy had trapped me into loving the warfare itself to the point where I was far out ahead of God in the battle, and the Lord had to call me to come back! You have to be led of God, even in doing spiritual things for Him. Many things appear to be "God things," but they are really only worldly or spiritual "good" things that are not in the Father's will.

I was at a Burger King one morning when a woman came in and said there was a guy sitting out in the middle of the road, yelling at nobody in particular. I thought to myself, "This I have got to see." So I got my breakfast and walked outside, and sure enough, there was some guy sitting right in the middle of the road where there was hardly any traffic. He was just sitting there, yelling to nobody. Then he got up and ran as fast as he could about ten steps, and then he sat back down as fast as he could and started yelling again.

I said to myself, "This guy is out of his mind." Then the thought came to me: if he was not in his mind, who *was* in his mind? Then I asked the Lord, "Well, Lord, do you want me to take care of this?" At that moment I felt that the Lord just wanted me to go to work because He was going to take care of the guy. As soon as I started heading to my truck, another thought came to me: *I thought you were some super demon-caster-outer. I thought you were some big sword-slinger for the Lord. How come you're not handling that?* And I replied, "Well, God told me to go to work, so shut up." And off to work I went. Just because somebody has a demon or a sickness, or just because there is an act of the Enemy, you're not under any obligation to do anything about it unless God wants you to. If the Lord is Lord, *follow* Him, don't get out ahead of Him.

Will God Answer Your Prayers?

A lot of people say that God doesn't answer all prayers, and that you never know what God will do. I looked into that, because when you get into spiritual warfare and you're praying, you're praying a lot. You'd better *know* that God is going to answer your prayer. I had to find out what God had to say about answering prayer. Here are some things I found.

"The prayer of the upright is God's delight" (Proverbs 15:9).

"God loves him that follows after righteousness" (Proverbs 15:8).

"God hears the prayers of the righteous" (Proverbs 15:29).

"The eyes of the Lord are over the righteous and his ears are opened unto their prayers" (1 Peter 3:12).

"The righteous are delivered out of trouble" (Proverbs 11:8).

"The righteous shall flourish like a branch" (Proverbs 11:20).

"Behold [look here] the righteous shall be rewarded in the earth" (Proverbs 11:31).

"Be not unequally yoked together with unbelievers for what fellowship hath righteousness with unrighteousness?" (2 Corinthians 6:14).

You can see that God delights in answering the prayers of the righteous. The Bible says in Hebrews 10:22 that "let us draw near with a true heart in full assurance of faith, having our hearts sprinkled from an evil conscience and our bodies washed with pure water." You have a conscious mind and a subconscious mind. One of the things I tell people all the time is to get to where they can consciously feel the presence of the Holy Spirit and never leave that place. When you can feel God, you have faith in Him because He's there. Your faith in what you believe and your conscience, mixed together with the word of God and the presence of the Holy Spirit, keep you living in the spiritual realm of God's kingdom by the power of the Holy Ghost. When it comes to doing spiritual warfare, the Bible says, "Behold, I give you the authority to trample on serpents and scorpions, and over all the power of the enemy, and nothing shall by any means hurt you." (Luke 10:19). Is that true or not? This is where you need to get to and then ask yourself, "Do I really believe God's word?"

Can You Trust God?

I read an article that told about an occasion when Pastor John Hagee was ministering. A guy walked up to him, stuck a gun in his face, and told him to beg for his life. John Hagee's answer was, "No weapon formed against me shall prosper. I will not beg for my life." The guy opened fire, point-blank, and missed every shot. When the police came and traced the locations where the bullets hit, they discovered an outline of wings.

When God says that nothing shall by any means hurt you, why should you fear? If the devil can't hurt you, what are you afraid of? Maybe you're thinking, *The devil is a fallen archangel, and he has all this power.* But what are you chopped liver? The Bible says in 1John 4:4 "You are of God, little children, and have overcome them (demons), because He who is in you is greater than he who is in the world." So, where is your faith? Do you have faith that Christ is in you, that in all these things you are more than a conqueror, that you have all power and authority over all the powers of the Enemy, that nothing shall by any means hurt you? That is what is says in Luke 10:19 "Behold, I give you the authority to trample on serpents and scorpions, and over all the power of the enemy, and nothing shall by any means hurt you." God says in Mathew 10:7,8, "And as you go, preach, saying, 'The kingdom of heaven is at hand.' Heal the sick, cleanse the lepers, raise the dead, cast out demons. Freely you have received, freely give."

Where is your faith? Where have you put it: in God's word or the world's circumstances? The Holy Spirit makes the word of God come alive in you so that the word of God in you can do what that word says it can do. Without the Spirit, the word is simply *logos*, or that which can be understood logically. The problem is that the logic of man is foolishness to God, and the logic of God is foolishness to man. The words in the Bible without the Spirit cannot be understood; they don't make sense, they are spirit. It takes the Spirit of God to turn the word of God from *logos* to *rhema*, which is the spoken word, the word becoming alive and real. Here's the difference. If you read a text on your phone, you may not be able to understand the true meaning behind it. If someone texts "I'll see you later," is that person saying he'll be glad to see you, or is he being confrontational? Without hearing the person say it, we can only assume what it means. The same is true for the Bible. If we just read it without the Holy Spirit revealing the meaning, we may take the scripture totally out of context. The Holy Spirit will reveal the context of what the word says. When you understand the word, you can then trust it, because the Holy Spirit not only reveals the context but also reveals the truth of the scripture.

The Lord spoke to me one time and said, "Since you are righteous, why do you function as a man instead of as my child?" This is where you have to understand yourself as a person. You are not your flesh; you are not even your own soul. You are a spirit that has a soul and lives in a body. You have to fight spiritual things from a spiritual place with the understanding of who you are in Christ and who Christ is in you. There is no separation between you and God. The devil will try to make you think, believe, and have faith that you are here on earth and God is in the third heaven, way up there. Nothing could be further from the truth. Yes, the Father is on His throne in heaven, and Jesus Christ is at the right hand of the Father, but where is the Holy Spirit? He's here!

Is there any difference between God the Father, God the Son, and God the Holy Spirit? No, they're all one, but they're separately three. I am a stepfather, a son, and myself. But these three are one, for I am the same person. The Trinity of the Father, Son, and Holy Ghost make up the Godhead, which is who God is. They are all God, and the God who created everything is in you. If you have been born again and baptized with the Holy Spirit. He has given you the power, through your faith in Jesus Christ and what He did on the cross at Calvary, to become a child of God. It is from that place, from that power and authority, that you exercise dominion over all the works of God's hands, as described in Genesis 1.

Can you name anything that God did not create? He has given you power and authority over all the creation of His hands, including heaven, earth, and the things under the earth, so that at the name of Jesus everything shall bow—but only when we are in the image and likeness of God as we were created to be (Genesis 1:26).

Do you remember or have any idea what happened at the Battle of the Bulge in World War II? The US military inserted US Army airborn in a place called Bastogne. The American soldiers were running out of food and ammunition, and they were completely surrounded by the Germans. Before going into Bastogne, the Americans had been told that they would be surrounded, and their response had been, "We're airborne. We're supposed to be surrounded." They didn't shy away from the fight. They were willing to lay down their lives for their country. Are we willing to lay down our lives for our country: the kingdom of God? What if the airborne rangers had been told ahead of time that General Patton was going to be able to take his tanks and bust through the German lines and save them? Would there have been any fear or worry? No! These soldiers had faith that they were going to go in there and hold that area until the rest of the army punched through and got to them. That was where they applied their faith. When we go into a spiritual battle; whether it's against storms, sickness, poverty, or whatever, the Bible doesn't say we're not going to have a battle. It says we're going to win that battle if we stand faithful, if we stand on the word of God and handle things through the Spirit. This is where the Enemy is going to try to tell you that what you are facing is what is real and God is not.

Let's look at Elisha and his servant. His servant looked out and saw only the chariots of the enemy. Elisha looked out there and said, "And Elisha prayed, and said, "Lord, I pray, open his eyes that he may see." Then the Lord opened the eyes of the young man, and he saw. And behold, the mountain *was* full of horses and chariots of fire all around Elisha." (2 Kings 6:17).

The great thing about our numbers of them that are with us is that in the book of Hebrews 12:22 it says "But you have come to Mount Zion and to the city of the living God, the heavenly Jerusalem, to an innumerable company of angels," So those that are with us are so many that you can't even number them and they are there to help you. Hebrews 1:14 says, "Are they not all ministering spirits sent forth to minister for those who will inherit salvation?" A lot of times we pray for God to do this or that, but He has actually given us the power and authority to do that which we ask Him to do. He tells us that He gave us everything in heaven to back us up. He gave us His word, His angels, His power, and His authority. Do you remember what the word *authority* means? *Authority* means "the legal right to exercise power." We can only operate spiritual things spiritually. The Bible says, "that your faith should not be in the wisdom of men but in the power of God." (1 Corinthians 2:5). How much power does God have? He has all of it. Do you have faith in God's power? Do you have faith that God will give you His power? According to scripture, He already has, so why are you not exercising that power? Is it because of unbelief, fear, doubt, or not knowing the scriptures? Many of the scribes and Pharisees didn't know the scriptures. In Matthew 22:29 Jesus said, "Jesus answered and said to them, "You are mistaken, not knowing the Scriptures nor the power of God." Do you think the devil hasn't studied God's book, the Bible? He knows the book a lot better than we do, and that's exactly what he uses against us.

What If We Don't Believe?

Let's discuss unbelief for a moment. To believe is to accept what is true or real. *Belief* means "the acceptance of truth or actuality without certain proof or confidence." Matthew 19:26 tells us, "But Jesus looked at *them* and said to them, "With men this is impossible, but with God *all things are possible*.," but God will not break His word. When Jesus was in His own hometown it says what happens when people don't believe, "Now He did not do many mighty works there because of their unbelief." (Matthew 13:58). It wasn't God's purpose *not* to do powerful works, but there was no faith. The people there didn't believe. God wasn't going to do miracles and healings for them if they didn't have any faith and trust in Him.

In Hebrews 11:6 God said "But without faith *it is* impossible to please *Him,* for he who comes to God must believe that He is, and *that* He is a rewarder of those who diligently seek Him." Would you do favors for someone you are not pleased with? No? God didn't either. Matthew 17:20 tells of the disciples being unable to cast a demon out of a particular person. "So Jesus said to them, "Because of your unbelief (you couldn't cast it out); for assuredly, I say to you, if you have faith as a mustard seed, you will say to this mountain, 'Move from here to there,' and it will move; and nothing will be impossible for you. In Mark 9:20-26 Jesus healed a boy possessed by an impure spirit, but before He did, he said to the boy's father, "Then they brought him to Him. And when he saw Him, immediately the spirit convulsed him, and he fell on the ground and wallowed, foaming at the mouth. So He asked his father, "How long has this been happening to him?" And he said, "From childhood. And often he has thrown him both into the fire and into the water to destroy him. But if You can do anything, have compassion on us and help us. Jesus said to him, "If you can believe, all things *are* possible to him who believes." Immediately the father of the child cried out and said with tears, "Lord, I believe; help my unbelief!" When Jesus saw that the people came running together, He rebuked the unclean spirit, saying to it: "Deaf and dumb spirit, I command you, come out of him and enter him no more!" Then *the spirit* cried out, convulsed him greatly, and came out of him. This is where you get the two sides of the fence. As Christians, they believed, yet they had unbelief and were double-minded. James 1:6–8 says that a man should ask God in faith. " But let him ask in faith, with no doubting, for he who doubts is like a wave of the sea driven and tossed by the wind. For let not that man suppose that he will receive anything from the Lord; *he is* a double-minded man, unstable in all his ways."

What if you were to cast out unbelief? What would be left? The only thing that would be left is belief. Scripture talks about the threefold chord Ecclesiastes 4:12 "Though one may be overpowered by another, two can withstand him. And a threefold cord is not quickly broken." The devil knows that too, so he doesn't just send you one demon of unbelief; he sends you three consisting of doubt, fear, and unbelief. Faith says that the resurrection power of God has been given unto us. Doubt says, "What if you pray and it doesn't work?" Unbelief says that it isn't ever going to work. Fear says, "If you do it and it doesn't work, everyone is going to laugh at you, and you're going to look stupid." So, you have all these different thoughts in the battlefield of the mind coming against God's word. They are coming against you, and through your mind they are coming against God. One of the two is going to prove real: God's word or the devil's lies. Where are you going to place your faith? If the Lord is God, follow Him. Put your faith in His word. What does His word say? Mark 16:17,18 "And these signs will follow those who believe: In My name they will cast out demons; they will speak with new tongues; they will take up serpents; and if they drink anything deadly, it will by no means hurt them; they will lay hands on the sick, and they will recover." What if you lay hands on the sick and they don't recover? What does God's word say? Lay hands on the sick and they shall recover. How do they recover? When do they recover? It doesn't matter; it's not our job to know these things. He doesn't say to lay hands on them and they will recover only *if* you know when and how.

Do Not Doubt or Give Up!

Let's look at the prophet Elisha. He had sent his servant to go and raise up a woman's dead child. (2Kings 4:18 – 37) His servant came back and basically said that there was no life in the boy, that he was dead. Elisha didn't think that it hadn't worked because God was on vacation. He didn't tell the mother to bury her son and maybe God would give her another one. No, Elisha went and lay prostrate on that little boy, and when he got up, there was still no breath in the child. So Elisha did it again, and when he got up, the child was still dead. So he did it again. In other words, he wasn't going to take no for an answer, because that's what faith is. After the third time, the boy arose. Faith doesn't accept anything other than God's word. Faith doesn't leave room for doubt, fear, and unbelief. Faith is what God used to create everything.

So, where is faith? It's everywhere. The person who has made a table got an idea, applied his faith to that idea, got the stuff, and made the table. The table is the manifestation of somebody's faith. Revelation 13:8 says, "and all who dwell on the earth will worship him, everyone whose name has not been written before the foundation of the world in the book of life of the Lamb who was slain.." God planned everything in His head, knowing before the world even existed that Jesus would be crucified. He saw how it was going to work and applied His faith to His word, and the Holy Spirit created it with faith.

When Elijah cut off the heads of all the prophets of Baal in 1 Kings 18, Jezebel sent her servant to tell Elijah that by the same time tomorrow he would be as one of them. The scripture says, "Then he was afraid, and he arose and ran for his life and came to Beersheba, which belongs to Judah, and left his servant there" (1 Kings 19:3, emphasis added). Elijah actually saw himself getting killed. Here was a guy who had just finished pouring water all over a sacrifice, had the fire of God come down from heaven and lick up all the water and take the sacrifice, and had turned the whole nation of Israel back to God. Then some woman had sent a messenger, who had said one sentence to him—and he had run for his life. He ended up sitting under a juniper tree, praying, 1Kings 19:4 "But he himself went a day's journey into the wilderness and came and sat down under a broom tree. And he asked that he might die, saying, "It is enough; now, O Lord, take away my life, for I am no better than my fathers." What had happened to his faith? He had seen a vision in his mind and had come into agreement with the lie of the woman instead of rising up in faith and coming back to Jezebel with something like this: "Last time I looked, God came down and acted on my word, not your word. God said it wasn't going to rain till I said so, and you know what? It didn't! You had four hundred prophets and priests of Baal show up, and they couldn't even get a little fire started. My God showed up, poured fire from heaven, licked up everything, and turned the whole nation of Israel back to Him. And we just killed all your prophets. And now you're sending this guy, your servant, to tell me that I'm going to die? No, I don't think so."

Functioning Spiritually

Jesus said in John 14:12, "Most assuredly, I say to you, he who believes in Me, the works that I do he will do also; and greater *works* than these he will do, because I go to My Father." Are you doing anything greater than Jesus did? If not, do you think we have a little bit of growing we need to do in our faith? Maybe we need a little separation between us and the world. Do you think we need a little more accumulation of God in us? There is a price to be paid for that. God says in Mather 7:7,8, "Ask, and it will be given to you; seek, and you will find; knock, and it will be opened to you. For everyone who asks receives, and he who seeks finds, and to him who knocks it will be opened." When you go into prayer, do you just say the typical, "Oh, Father in heaven, here is my prayer. Answer it if you want. I don't know if you really will, but I'm kinda hoping you will"? Is this something that God is really going to honor? You may wonder why a lot of prayers don't get answered. It's not the absence of faith, because we've all been given a measure of faith; Romans 12:3, "For I say, through the grace given to me, to everyone who is among you, not to think *of himself* more highly than he ought to think, but to think soberly, as God has dealt to each one a measure of faith." It's the presence of unbelief. Unbelief is a demon spirit. The Bible tells us that God has not given us a spirit of fear, but of power, love, and a sound mind (2 Timothy 1:7). We can see that fear is a demonic spirit, but God has given us a spirit of power, a spirit of love, and a spirit of a sound mind. So, as God sends His angels with messages to us, the devil sends his messengers too, and we have a choice of which messenger to believe.

There are crazy people out there who have a spirit of an unsound mind, or, as the Bible sometimes calls it, *madness*. God has given us the spirit of a sound mind, and when something comes against our mind and tries to make us crazy, it isn't from God. We take authority over it by telling it that we refuse to entertain crazy thoughts or mental pressure because God has given us a sound mind. I rebuke that in Jesus's name. I do not come into agreement with it. You may know someone who is going crazy. The word *sick* means being oppressed by the Enemy, and scripture talks about being sick in the head, or oppressed in the mind. Well, if you've been given authority over all the power of the enemy so you can have the power to break that off of somebody, can you make it happen? Absolutely!

The Price of Manifestation

Kenneth Hagin had a church in Texas, and he was a faith preacher before he went to be with the Lord. He had three guys from his seminary school come to him and say, "We want to go to the insane asylum and restore somebody's mind." Pastor Hagin asked them if they were willing to pay the price it was going to take, because they would be dealing with powers, principalities, and spiritual wickedness in high places. The sort of spirit they would be dealing with depended on the kind of power the spirit had.

If you have one soldier of the enemy, and he's facing a hundred US Navy SEALs, how long is that battle going to last? Not long at all. If you take a hundred US Navy SEALs and send them against a whole country full of the enemy, how long is *that* battle going to last? As long as it takes until the SEALs win. So these three guys went and for three days laid hands on a guy in a battle for his mind. God restored the man's mind, and he was released from that asylum. Now faith also works for unbelievers. There was a guy in jail who had come down with a disease, and they told him he was going to die in prison. Something snapped in him, and he said to himself that this wasn't how he wanted his life to go, and he would not die in prison. He started going to school while in prison, became a lawyer, beat the disease, and got out of jail on parole—even though he had been there for a life sentence! He applied his faith to what he believed, and it manifested itself. He got out of prison, and he beat the disease. Now, if he had come into agreement with the words of the jailhouse doctor, he would have died in jail.

There is a spiritual law of agreement. Matthew 18:19 says that if two come into agreement in anything, it shall be done. You have to be very careful of what you agree with. That is why we need to know what the Bible says: so we can agree with it.

Faith and Works

A man named Naaman came to Elisha to be cured of leprosy (2 Kings 5:9), and Elisha told him to go and dip in the Jordan river seven times. How did Naaman respond? He grumbled and complained that the water was nasty and that Elisha should have come out to meet him and wave his hand over the leprosy. Naaman wasn't willing to do the action part. And what does scripture say about faith without works? It's dead! A lot of people say they have faith in God's word, but they don't apply God's word to anything. They got the ticket to heaven for believing Jesus died for them. That gives them entrance into heaven, but what have they done with God's word? There are so many people who read the Bible cover to cover but don't apply any of it or do anything spiritual with what they have been given.

When I first became born-again, my prayer was this: "Lord, show me everything I need to know now, because once I'm dead, I can't help anyone!" I read the scripture that says, "But God has revealed *them* to us through His Spirit. For the Spirit searches all things, yes, the deep things of God." (1 Corinthians 2:10). I said, "Well, Holy Spirit, take me with you." But then it has to come down to why you want to know such things. Why read the Bible? To feel good? It is the Sword of the Spirit. Why hold or even look at a sword if you're not going to cut anything with it. Does that make any sense? God gave us His word to use. You don't give a sword to a child; he'll hurt himself. You give a sword to somebody who has been trained to use it. So, our prayer should be this: "Lord, teach me Your word and what to do with it. Make me a master at using Your word for Your kingdom.

There are lots of different things we don't have faith in that we need to change our minds about. "He who is in me is greater than he who is in the world" (1 John 4:4). You can't just *hear* that; you have to *believe* it, because the Bible says that even the devils believe and tremble. And now you have to apply it. You have to know that he who is in you is greater than he who is in the world.

Who Has the Power?

A lot of people think that the devil has control of hell and death, but we can clearly see in Revelation 1:18 that Jesus has the keys of Hades (hell) and death. So, who has the power over death? Jesus does, and "as he is so are we in this world" (1 John 4:17). So, who has the power over death? We do. That is why Jesus commanded the disciples to go and cast out demons, lay hands on the sick, and raise the dead. He wouldn't have told them to do it if they didn't have the power and legal authority to do so.

I used to drink and do drugs before the Lord got ahold of me. When I was born again, the Lord had me lay hands on my own head to resurrect my brain cells. My memory came back, and the memory I have now can retain things far better than it did before. Jesus said, "Behold I give unto you power to tread on serpents and scorpions, and over all the power of the enemy: and nothing shall by any means hurt you" (Luke 10:19). The spirit of death and destruction that was on my mind was removed by the power of God, and my mind was restored. This same power is available through the Holy Spirit to destroy the works and spirits of the Enemy.

Dealing with the Devil and This World

In my next book I will go over the different demons and the deliverance sessions that God has done through my life and through me to set others free. But in this book I just want to give you the basis for understanding some things about the devil.

Sometimes the Enemy will say that bad things happen to you because of a curse. The curse is a spoken punishment for breaking God's law. The devil doesn't go by the law, for he's a lawbreaker, and we are the enforcers of God's word. If there is a curse, then we can use Galatians 3:13: "Christ has redeemed us from the curse of the law, having become a curse for us (for it is written, "Cursed *is* everyone who hangs on a tree"." Jesus took the curses that were meant for us when we break God's law. He put those curses on Himself and freed us from them. But what happens when the Enemy still tries to uphold that curse? Then you take Galatians 3:13 and remind Satan that you have been redeemed and bought with the highest price, the blood of Jesus Christ, and that He has cleansed you from that. When Jesus took your sin, which was not only the breaking of God's word but the penalty (curse), He bore that upon Himself. You can then command any demon working on that curse to cease and go where Jesus commands them to go. If you went out to dinner, and Jesus came by and paid your bill, but the server kept coming up and trying to hand you a bill, would you take it? If the Enemy keeps trying to give you a curse, are you going to take it? No! But there are many people out there who don't know about what Jesus has done for them, and they do this every day.

Overcoming the World

There are sins in the Bible for which the curse or judgment is poverty. Have you been redeemed? Sure! Now, there are different definitions of poverty. Paul said, "I know what it means to abase and abound, to have and to not have." *Poverty* means that you don't have what you need, and you're never going to get it. Paul says, "And my God shall supply all your need according to His riches in glory by Christ Jesus." When you don't have something, that just means you don't need it now. If you needed it, you would have it, because God said He would supply it. That's why Paul said, "In not having, I have all things. By not knowing, I know all things." Whatever Paul had need of, God was going to supply. Jesus took the twelve disciples and sent them out in Mark 6:7-9, "And He called the twelve to *Himself,* and began to send them out two *by* two, and gave them power over unclean spirits. He commanded them to take nothing for the journey except a staff—no bag, no bread, no copper in *their* money belts, but to wear sandals, and not to put on two tunics." Why would Jesus do that? Because He had to build their faith that no matter what they needed, God was going to supply it. What does fear say? "I don't have it, I'm never going to have it, and the world is going to overcome me." But scripture states, " For whatever is born of God overcomes the world. And this is the victory that has overcome the world our faith." (1 John 5:4). Do you think when we get to heaven we're going to have to pay a mortgage on a house? No! So I would assume a mortgage is a worldly thing, right? Is that mortgage going to overcome us, or are we going to apply our faith to God's word, which says that if we need to pay that mortgage, God will supply what we need, and that mortgage will get paid.

What happens if the mortgage doesn't get paid? Then you don't need to pay it. What if the house gets foreclosed on, and you get removed from that house? Then maybe that was exactly what you needed. God may have something bigger and better for you, but until you get out of that house, He can't give it to you. God's ways are not our ways. They do not make sense to man, but in the end, we can see God's wisdom if we just trust Him. We must also understand that without God's righteousness we cannot partake of His promises. We cannot walk in sin and expect to be blessed.

Years ago I was working in restaurants. If you had told me then that I would get hired as a professional photographer and start a photography business that would introduce me to three hundred realtors and open up the door for a home inspection business, and that I would be one of the busiest, most sought-after, successful home inspection businesses, and that I would then become a pastor of a church, I would have told you that you had lost your mind. There were no signs of any open doors that led to that path, but that was exactly the path the Lord laid out for me. I got hired as a professional photographer to take photos of real estate, without ever owning a camera or taking a class on photography.

You see, God isn't limited to our knowledge and abilities. If He wants us to do something, He will give us the ability and knowledge when we need it. Within a very short time, in a business that had quite a few photographers, all the realtors were requesting me to do their photos. It was through meeting all of the realtors that I was able to open a home inspection business, and God's word, which says that He orders the steps of the righteous, has come to pass in my life.

Whatever is going on, have faith in God that He will work things out for your benefit. Those who put their faith in the Lord shall not be ashamed (Isaiah 49:23). Stay spiritually connected to God.

Our Relationship with God

How is it possible to have a relationship with God? The Bible tells us how we can have a relationship with the Father, Jesus, and the Holy Ghost. It explains that "Therefore, having been justified by faith, we have peace with God through our Lord Jesus Christ," (Romans 5:1). When we receive Jesus's sacrifice for us and allow Him to be Lord of our lives, all our sins are forgiven.

Romans 3:23 says that all have sinned and fallen short of the glory of God, being justified freely by His grace through the redemption that is in Christ Jesus. Every one of us is born a sinner. It's in our blood and travels through us, just like the genetics that give us blue or brown eyes and blonde or brown hair.

So, how does this freeing us from the power of sin happen? Romans 3:23 lets us know that it is not of our own doing. "for all have sinned and fall short of the glory of God," Romans 3:27 "Where *is* boasting then? It is excluded. By what law? Of works? No, but by the law of faith." It is excluded. It is excluded because there is nothing you can do yourself to make this freedom happen. What frees us from the power of sin? The works you can do? No, it is the law of faith that frees us.

The Law of Faith

The law of works is based on what you can do yourself. The law of faith *believes* in someone else—who that person is, and what that person says and does and can do for you. Therefore, we conclude—or come to the understanding and accept—that a man is justified by faith apart from works. You have to understand that this is everything your Father in heaven does for you, and He does it by showing grace through His love for us. We can't do it ourselves, and He did it because He wants a relationship with us. It was only through the crucifixion and punishment of Jesus for us that were we able to be freed from the power of sin so the Father could have a relationship with us. All we need to do for our part is to believe it and walk it out. This is where other "religions" miss it. They have no way of separating sin from themselves. We cannot do anything to make this happen ourselves, which is why the Bible says that it is not of works (the things we do) but of faith (in what He does). If you are reading this and do not have a relationship with God, then speak these words aloud to Him before reading further. "Father, I do not know if this is real or not. Since I am reading this, I am seeking to know the truth about you, and I ask you to give me understanding and prove to me that Your word is true. Please come into my life and have a relationship with me.

Knowing God

It's all wrapped up in what you know and whom you know. When you begin to know what the word of God says, you start to get an idea about the one who said it. When you know Him, you can then have understanding, knowledge, and faith in Him that what He says is truth. Then you can have faith in Him and the power of His words.

God and His word are one. The Bible says in John 1: In the beginning was the Word, and the Word was with God, and the Word was God." And in John 1:14 "And the Word became flesh and dwelt among us, and we beheld His glory, the glory as of the only begotten of the Father, full of grace and truth." The Word became flesh and dwelt among men in the form of Jesus Christ. You cannot have faith in someone's words without having faith in the one who spoke them. The scribes and Pharisees knew what the Torah (the first five books of the Bible) said, but they didn't know God, the one who had spoken them. God longs to have an intimate relationship with all people, but all people will not accept Him as God, so He lets them go and worship whatever else they want. But to those who choose to allow Him to have a relationship with them, He proves beyond a shadow of a doubt that He is the one and only God. That is why the Bible says that you will be a witness. A witness is someone who sees or hears and can testify to the truth of what they know. In believing God and having a relationship with Him, you will be a witness of Him.

Being a Child of God

Jesus asked a question: "But He answered and said to the one who told Him, "Who is My mother and who are My brothers?" And He stretched out His hand toward His disciples and said, "Here are My mother and My brothers! For whoever does the will of My Father in heaven is My brother and sister and mother." (Mathew 12:48-50) What is the will of the Father that we are supposed to be doing? Jesus answered and said to them, "This is the work of God, that you believe in Him whom He sent." (John 6:29). He asked the question about who His mother and brothers were when Jesus's mother and brothers were coming for Him,. His mother and brothers were coming to get Him, because they believed He had gone mad and was crazy. They did not believe in Him as the Messiah and Son of God, and therefore they were not doing the will of God. Jesus asked the people, "But why do you call Me 'Lord, Lord,' and not do the things which I say? (Luke 6:46). In Matthew, chapters 5 through 8, Jesus revealed to us what we need to do to enter into the straight gate of the kingdom of heaven (the spiritual kingdom of God). Jesus said in Matthew 5:22 " But I say to you that whoever is angry with his brother without a cause shall be in danger of the judgment. And whoever says to his brother, 'Raca (calling him worthless)!' shall be in danger of the council. But whoever says, 'You fool!' shall be in danger of hell fire." After accepting Jesus as Lord and being filled with the Holy Spirit, if we have any problems with a brother, we are to go to him and work it out and not allow unforgiveness to gain a hold on us. In verse 27 He talked about adultery, meaning that if someone had a problem with a spouse, the person was to handle it and not go to the arms of someone else. In verse 5:29 He said "If your right eye causes you to sin, (makes you angry) pluck it out and cast *it* from you; for it is more profitable for you that one of your members perish, than for your whole body to be cast into hell.

Now, He wasn't saying to really remove your eye! He was saying that if you see something that makes you angry, stop looking at it. God does the same thing when we walk in sin: He turns His head from us. Jesus also went on to say that if our hand offends us, we are to cut it off. If we see or do something that makes us angry, we are to remove our hand from it. In verse 44 He even went so far as to tell us to love our enemy. In doing these things we can then rely on verse 45, which tells us that in doing so, we will be the children of our Father in heaven. It is by being a child of God that we enter into the straight gate and into the kingdom of heaven. As Jesus was on the cross, He asked the Father to forgive the people for what they were doing, because they didn't realize what they were doing. People do things without godly understanding.

In Matthew 6 we are instructed not to do things for man's acceptance or for worldly gain but to do everything for God. Verse 21 says "For where your treasure is, there your heart will be also." God is saying that the things that mean the most to you are the things you have a heartfelt attachment to. The first of the Ten Commandments says to love the Lord your God with all your heart. If you have things and people that you value more than God, then you are walking in sin. When you get your heart right with God, you have direct access to Him through the Spirit.

Matthew 7:8 explains that when you are right with God, "For everyone who asks receives, and he who seeks finds, and to him who knocks it will be opened." Whatever you ask shall be granted; whatever you seek, you will find. He says that many will want to enter in but will not be able to because their hearts are not right toward God. They are walking in unforgiveness and anger and are choosing to hold onto that instead of holding onto God. In Matthew 7:21 God said, "Not everyone who says to Me, 'Lord, Lord,' shall enter the kingdom of heaven, but he who does the will of My Father in heaven." He will not allow those who walk in sin to enter his kingdom. Just as Jesus asked the Father to forgive, we need to forgive also.

In Matthew 10:25 God said, "It is enough for a disciple that he be like his teacher, and a servant like his master. If they have called the master of the house Beelzebub, (king of demons) how much more *will they call* those of his household!" We are supposed to be as much a child of God as Jesus is and do the things that Jesus did and the people of the world and the demons of Satan's kingdom will try to stop us by calling us names, and saying we are the crazy ones. In Matthew 10:7 Jesus told His disciples "And as you go, preach, saying, 'The kingdom of heaven is at hand. Heal the sick, cleanse the lepers, raise the dead, cast out demons. Freely you have received, freely give." These are the things that happen to and through a child of God.

It is God's will for us to obey all of God's law, but He understands that we need to be cleansed of all unrighteousness to do that. It is during the cleansing process that the Lord allows all our faults, hurts, and demons to manifest so we can deal with them and clean them out of our lives. And until we are completely set free and renewed to be His child, He gives us grace.

The Transformation

Now in believing that Jesus is the Son of God, there comes a transformation within you that will change who you are down to the very core. To those who believe, He has given the power to become sons and daughters of God (John 1:12).

What does it mean to be a son? As a son or daughter, we are to take on the Father's attributes and show that He is in us through the same Spirit that is in Him. That is why we need to be spiritually born again. Then it is the Spirit of God (the Holy Spirit) who lives in us. Matthew 11:11 states "Assuredly, I say to you, among those born of women there has not risen one greater than John the Baptist; but he who is least in the kingdom of heaven is greater than he." The ones in the kingdom are the ones who have been born again spiritually. John told Jesus, "saying, "I need to be baptized by You, and are You coming to me?" (Matthew 3:14), but he never was. It was not in God's plan. Those of us who believe that Jesus is the Son of God need another thing besides being baptized for forgiveness of sins. We need to be baptized in the Holy Spirit. That is the baptism that John wanted from Jesus.

When I first started going to church and couldn't really understand the Bible, the Lord kept bringing me to the book of Acts. In Acts 1:4–5 Jesus told the disciples to wait for the promise of the baptism of the Holy Spirit, and in verse 8 He said they would receive power and be a witness of Jesus, seeing proof of who He was. In Matthew 3:11 John said that Jesus would baptize believers with the Holy Ghost and fire. Since it is Jesus who baptizes, I prayed to Jesus and told Him that I accepted Him as my Lord and Savior. I asked Him to baptize me in His Holy Spirit, from the crown of my head to the souls of my feet, and I thanked Him for it. After about a day or two, I started to hear His voice in my head and spirit, and I felt Him lead me to read the Bible. I was understanding everything and getting such revelation from what I was reading. About two weeks after I prayed, the gift of tongues came over me. It started out by just speaking sylabols of "ta ta ta ta," and then I went off in a language that I had no understanding of. I had no thought about speaking it, but it was coming out of my mouth. I found through the years different dialects coming through my mouth. I know at one point it was French sounding and at one point it turned to something like Chinese. I prayed for the Lord to change it because every time I prayed in the spirit, in Chinese it would make me laugh. He was accommodating and it went back to my original language. There are times I would pray in the spirit and ask the Holy Ghost to reveal to my mind what it is that was being spoken. One of the gifts that the Holy Spirit bestows on people is the interpretation of tongues. (1Corinthians 12:10)

For about a year and a half, I could not get enough of the word of God in the Bible. God was showing me all kinds of wondrous things, and in my everyday life He was speaking to me, showing me miracles, and doing miracles through me for others. People would get healed of all kinds of things, and miracles of other kinds were also being done. The Holy Spirit is such a wonderful person, and I cherish my relationship with Him. Through

Him flows God's love for me, and for others through me. He makes me love Him with all my heart.

From a Child to a Servant

There are many parables in scripture that point to different kinds of people. There are servants, friends, family, and enemies listed throughout scripture. Paul said he was a bond servant in the book of Romans, an apostle and bond servant in many of the epistles, and a prisoner of Christ in the epistle of Philemon. James also called himself a bond servant in his epistle. Peter called himself a bond servant in his second epistle. Jude called himself a bond servant in his epistle. A bond servant is one who serves without getting paid and is in bondage to his master for the rest of his life by choice. When one loves his master with his whole heart, pleasing his master is payment enough, and pleasing his master is what he lives for. Although it is called a bond servant, the servant is neither in bondage nor slavery. In serving his master, he is attaining his heart's desire. Why would anyone want to be a bond servant to someone? How could a person love so much that he would serve and do his master's will for his entire life without caring about reward or payment? Is it possible that his love for his master pales in comparison to the love the master has for him? This is where the family connection comes in. When we are in unison and obedient to the Spirit of God, we become family. Even though God is God, and Jesus is Lord, He is not ashamed to call us brethren, because we all have the same spirit (Hebrews 2:11). What if, in serving the master, the gifts and rewards were greater and more valuable than any other master would ever come close to giving? The servant's knowledge and appreciation for what the master does for him and of the love given by them, (The Father, Jesus, and The Holy Spirit) for the younger children (us) and us being aware of it makes us love the master back. God pours out His love on us so we can know what His love is and partake in it, and that has changed us. We love Christ, for He first loved us. Even when were dead in sins (Ephesians 2:5), He died for us, freeing us from the wrath that is to come on all those who deny Him.

The Trap of Losing Focus

Many people fall away from being the bond servant of Christ, because they lose sight of why they became a bond servant to begin with. They start to focus on servanthood and the jobs and frustrations of the jobs instead of staying focused on the one they are working for and the reason they work for Him. There are only two masters, God and the devil, and you will serve one or the other.

The devil deceives you into thinking you are your own master, filling you with a false sense of pride. Satan places his interests and desires in you and then makes you believe they are your own desires. Then you choose his will, thinking it is your own will. In believing that you are the master, you believe that you are in charge and can make the rules and do as you chose. You believe that there are no consequences to the decisions you make, because you are the only one you have to answer to, or in your pride, you are deceived into thinking that you will not be found out or caught. These are the people who do not believe in God. The truth is that in choosing Satan's will, you get the judgments pronounced by God upon Satan for his will and actions. As a parent, would you not discipline your child for being disobedient? These are the curses and judgments that are listed throughout scripture. I have ministered to many people who were deceived into thinking that they could live their own lives, and even doing that, they were never happy. There was always a hole in them they couldn't fill, and they were always tormented by never having that completeness that comes from God's filling the void. He created that void in us that only He can fill. The devil will try to get you to fill that void with money, sex, drugs, alcohol, and a host of other things always knowing that these will never work, but he is laughing about the destruction those things bring into your life.

Satan's Servants and God's Servants

Satan imparts his spirits (demons) into people, sometimes before they are even born. Scripture states that the sins of the fathers are visited unto the children to the third and fourth generation. (Numbers 14:18, Exodus 20:5, Exodus 34:7) That is why we see so many people following in the footsteps of their parents. Satan has a plan and a use for all his servants to accomplish his will, which is to do nothing but steal, kill, and destroy (John 10:10). God allows people to be used by Satan first so they can see what kind of master he is. Then they can choose to serve God when they see what kind of master He is. God sees all people and has chosen which ones are going to be His. He calls many, but few are chosen (Mathew 22:14). Many will not choose God because of fear, ignorance, falsehoods about God, or not having a complete separation from the kingdom of Satan and then trying to serve two masters. Some have become addicted to the desires (sins) that are fed in Satan's kingdom, and they don't want to give them up. Some have become addicted to drugs, sex, food, and other things that make them "feel good," and they don't want to give them up. Or the demons that now control their will and thoughts will not let them quit, and in the end they lead to sickness and disease, poverty, and death.

God's servants are direct representatives of Himself. In order to be a servant of His, you must have some qualities that qualify you. This is the training that happens after one has chosen to be a child/servant of God. You will need to be trained in faith, holiness, righteousness, love, and warfare as well as many other aspects required to function within God's kingdom. If you think about the purity that is in God's kingdom—no lies, evil designs, or evil speaking; and all thoughts, speech, and actions being done in righteousness and holiness—you can see where we have a long way to go. But God gives us grace while we are on that path of spiritual growth.

We will now look at the contrast between servants of God and servants of Satan. As stated earlier, God's servants are direct representatives of Him. Thus Satan's servants are direct representatives of him. In the contrasts, we see that God is truth, and Satan is a liar who uses truth and mixes in a little lie to distort the truth. God has bound Himself to integrity by binding Himself to His word. Satan has no problem going back on his word and has no integrity. God is the giver of life and the sustainer of it. Satan is the destroyer of life and killer of it. God blesses those who bless Him, for eternity. Satan hates and cares nothing for people and gives to his servants to only to get what he wants—and then he takes more than he gives. Satan may give wealth, power, and earthly prestige, but at the end of life, it costs you your soul and complete separation from God and everlasting torment. Since Satan only cares about himself, you can see that same selfish attitude in his followers. One of the greatest contrasts between God and Satan is this: love gives, and hate takes. In this we see that God is love 1John 4:8 "He who does not love does not know God, for God is love." because He is always giving, whereas Satan is hate-filled. Satan cares for no one and especially does not care for or about God, God's creation, and especially God's children. In the end God pronounces judgment on those who follow Satan 2Peter 2:4-10 "For if God did not spare the angels who sinned, but cast *them* down to hell and delivered *them* into chains of darkness, to be reserved for judgment; and did not spare the ancient world, but saved Noah, *one of* eight *people*, a preacher of righteousness, bringing in the flood on the world of the ungodly; and turning the cities of Sodom and Gomorrah into ashes, condemned *them* to destruction, making *them* an example to those who afterward would live ungodly; and delivered righteous Lot, *who was* oppressed by the filthy conduct of the wicked (for that righteous man, dwelling among them, tormented *his* righteous soul from day to day by seeing and hearing *their* lawless deeds) *then* the Lord knows how to deliver the godly out of temptations and to reserve the unjust under punishment for the day of judgment, and especially those who walk according to the flesh in the lust of uncleanness and despise authority. *They are* presumptuous, self-willed." because they have followed the ways of evil and have not accepted His Son's sacrifice for sins. Therefore, they must pay the price for their sins. When you receive, and accept Jesus as your payment for sins, and you choose to live for Him, God makes you righteous because you have faith in what He did through Jesus. This is a gift that you have to just accept, for you can't earn it or buy it. As God's servant, you extend that same love, grace, and compassion to others so that they may see God in you and through you.

The Blessing

What can you look forward to by being a bond servant or child of God? First, He will never leave you nor forsake you (Deuteronomy 31:6) Earthly parents leave and abandon children, and I pray that yours did not, but if they have, know that your heavenly Father never will. He longs to be with you, share His life with you, and have you share your life with Him. In being His servant/child, you will not only get paid, but as a good boss or parent treats His workers, you will get bonuses that you did not know He was giving. What are these payments and bonuses? God has made a contract for those who choose to be His servants, and He has signed it and sealed it in His own blood through the death of His Son. He has vowed to bless you with joy, happiness, fulfillment, substance, and relationships. He has even decreed to give you Himself in the form of the Holy Spirit and to infuse you with His power, which is all-powerful. He will impart His wisdom and understanding into your mind and lead you and guide you on where to go, what to do, and what to say. He has promised this for all of eternity, and it will never end. All He requires is that you serve Him with your whole heart and be obedient to what He says and wants you to do, because what good is a son/servant who doesn't do what his Father/master wants?

Unforgiveness: The Destroyer of Relationships

There is one other area that needs to be discussed. Faith is the way that we can have a relationship with God, but it is sin that broke the relationship in the first place. Since Jesus forgave our sins and took them and God's punishment upon Himself, He now requires something from us in order to keep that grace and forgiveness. Matthew 18:34,35 says, "And his master was angry, and delivered him to the torturers until he should pay all that was due to him. So My heavenly Father also will do to you if each of you, from his heart, does not forgive his brother his trespasses."

The devil fights with us, tooth and nail, to try to get us hurt, offended, angry, and bitter toward people so that we will not forgive them. In doing so, he knows that our unforgiveness will cause a break in our relationship with God, and God will fulfill His word by allowing the devil to torment us until we forgive. I have ministered to many people who have a root of bitterness that has led to unforgiveness, and they have come to me because their lives are full of trouble and problems. Bitterness is a poison that flows through the soul and poisons the heart and arteries. It causes hardening of the heart and artery walls and causes heart attacks and strokes. Bitterness releases stress, and stress takes an enormous toll on the body. The heart is like a sponge. It is supposed to soak up love for itself, and then the excess is supposed to flow through it to others. When the heart becomes hard, then love won't flow into it or through it. Scripture states that faith works by love (Galatians 5:6). The devil knows that if you do not love, God cannot flow through you, for God is love (1 John 4:8). God is justified in this. Is it right for Him to forgive you but then not to require you also to forgive, especially since He is God? In keeping our hearts right with God, we become the desire of His heart. He pours His blessings upon us, and our relationship with Him through Christ is secured.

How to Walk with God

As you journey on your walk with Christ, you will become more and more the manifestation of the child of God, just as it says in Psalms 82:6 "I said, "You *are* gods, And all of you *are* children of the Most High." The Enemy is going to try to derail you from being that godly child. That is why the Lord gave that whole speech about being offended. He told us that if our eye offends us, we're to cut it out. If our arm offends us, we are to cut it off. So, what is the plan of the Enemy? To get you offended. Why? Well, you should remember that he knows scripture, so he is going to use God's promises against us, just as we are supposed to use God's promises for us and against the Enemy. Satan knows that if you do not forgive, then neither will your Father in heaven forgive you. The rest of God's promise says that since you will not forgive, you will be handed over to the tormentors. What is the plan of the Enemy? To use your disobedience to God's word to torment you, and as he is tormenting you, he will blame it on God.

Baggage

When you become born again, you're all happy and have a big smile on your face. As you are traveling along on your walk with God, the Enemy send you some baggage, hoping you'll pick it up and carry it. Somebody in the church gets envious of you and your happiness, and they say something against you, and it causes an emotional wound to you. Basically, it hurts your feelings. The wound of envy hurts your heart, because people should love you instead of speaking evil to or about you. Then, as you are traveling, maybe you find somebody in the church you think you can confide in. Maybe it concerns something on which the Lord is dealing with you. You go to this person and tell him of your struggle, and instead of the being in the love of Christ (where there is no condemnation for those in Christ), this person turns around and tells everybody. So now everybody knows about your business. You become ashamed and hurt. You pick up another piece of baggage, that of being wounded by gossip. Now you are walking with the Lord, and instead of walking hand in hand with Him, you are carrying two suitcases of pain, shame, and emotional wounds. You are starting to ask yourself, "Okay, why is my walk with God not going like it should be going?" You are now carrying wounds of gossip and envy.

And then the preacher tells you, "If you are not inviting five people to church every week, and if you are not tithing 10 percent of your entire income every week, if you are not serving in all the areas of the church by scrubbing toilets and doing every ministry of "helps," if you are not helping grow the church—then you are just not living right for God." Adding to the wounds of gossip and envy, you have now picked up the feeling and belief that you are unworthy because you are not "doing" everything you can for the church and those feelings come from spirits of unworthiness and guilt which are tools of the enemy to try and control you. If any of these have been found in your life, then go into prayer and ask the Holy Spirit to remove any guilt, shame, condemnation or unworthiness that may be afflicting you and to lead you in what He wants you to do.

Removing Baggage

So, now you've become wounded through condemnation. You're walking with God, but you are now loaded down like a pack mule with hurts, pains, unforgiveness, and unworthiness instead of walking in the freedom to enjoy life with Christ. You are walking around like a mule, struggling under the weight of all this demonic baggage of bad thoughts that you have accepted and now have on your shoulders. What has happened to you as you are walking? All this emotional and mental baggage you are carrying will manifest on the outside of you. The problem is that we don't know what we are supposed to what with all this stuff. God knows what being this way does to us, so he tells us in His word how to handle it. We are to be "casting all your care upon Him, for He cares for you." (1 Peter 5:7), and as Paul says, "Brethren, I do not count myself to have apprehended; but one thing *I do,* forgetting those things which are behind and reaching forward to those things which are ahead," (Philippians 3:13). We cannot go forward in Christ and carry all this baggage with us. That is why the Bible says it is easier for a camel to go through the eye of a needle than it is for a rich man to enter into the kingdom of God. What is the eye of the needle? The eye of the needle is a gate in the city wall that the camels went through to get into the city. It is only big enough for the camel to go through after everything it has been carrying has been unloaded from it. The gate is only big enough for *you* to walk through, and you cannot walk through it carrying any baggage. The teaching about the eye of the needle is that we have to allow all that stuff to be removed from us in order to enter God's gate and reside in His presence. It is only by getting to the root of the feelings and confronting them that we can be set free and released from them. Many people don't remember where the baggage came from or why they have it. If you ask the Holy Spirit to reveal to you why you feel or think a certain way, he will reveal it to you.

This is how we are supposed to walk with God. We are to trust that He will take care of those who have tried to hurt us or condemn us. We are to stay unburdened by anything that people and Satan try to put on us. We are only supposed to carry the Lord's burden and what He wants us to carry. We are to cast (throw) our cares upon Him. He bore all of our cares on Himself on the cross of Calvary when He died for us. We are not supposed to be carrying this stuff. When something comes up in you that has either happened to you in the past or was spoken to you or about you, you have to let it go. Get rid of it. It may be something that you just need healing from. It may not necessarily be a demon spirit afflicting you. It may be just a wound that hurt you on a previous occasion that you have never dealt with, and so you have carried it your entire life. It might even have occurred before your life with Christ, because before Christ, lots of stuff happens to us. Did you accept Christ and bring all that with you? When you move into someone else's house, do you bring all your belongings with you? No. What do you do? You bring the things that you need for life and godliness. I would hope that you would bring your Bible. That would be the "godliness" part. Then you would need clothes, a toothbrush, and that kind of stuff. As we go forward in our life with Christ, let's take all the stuff that happened to us before we knew Him, and cast it into the sea of forgetfulness. God has. Micah 7:19 "He will again have compassion on us, And will subdue our iniquities. You will cast all our sins Into the depths of the sea." And Hebrews 8:12 "For I will be merciful to their unrighteousness, and their sins and their lawless deeds I will remember no more." How can you do that? Great question. I have read many books that tell you to do stuff, but they never tell you how. My prayer is that this book will give you the directions as well as the pieces of the puzzle.

Let's say that you recognize one of those burdens. Your prayer can go something like this: "Lord, I lay down my burden at Your feet. This is what I feel, and this is what happened. I am going to trust in You and forgive all who have hurt me (be as specific as possible), and I pray that You will heal me right now of these wounds and pain. Holy Spirit, come into me and take the place of these things inside me."

Then God says, "Okay, let's go over here." Don't pick those burdens back up and take them with you. Don't let the Enemy remind you of what happened back there. That was why Peter asked in Mathew 18:21,22 Then Peter came to Him and said, "Lord, how often shall my brother sin against me, and I forgive him? Up to seven times?" Jesus said to him, "I do not say to you, up to seven times, but up to seventy times seven. And the Lord said, "Not seven but seventy times seven. Why? Because that is how many times the Enemy is going to bring that back to you to try to get you offended and in unforgiveness. Your answer every time a thought comes up to try to upset you, you need to say, "I forgave them before, and I forgive them still, and I am going to forgive them and forgive them until the Enemy stops bringing it back to me." You cannot allow offense to reign within you. It will destroy or greatly hinder your walk with God.

The Council of God

"For who has stood in the counsel of the LORD, And has perceived and heard His word? Who has marked His word and heard *it?* Behold, a whirlwind of the LORD has gone forth in fury— A violent whirlwind! It will fall violently on the head of the wicked. The anger of the LORD will not turn back until He has executed and performed the thoughts of His heart. In the latter days you will understand it perfectly. "I have not sent these prophets, yet they ran. I have not spoken to them, yet they prophesied. But if they had stood in My counsel, and had caused My people to hear My words, Then they would have turned them from their evil way and from the evil of their doings." (Jeremiah 23:18, 22).

God is looking for people to have a relationship with Him so that He can talk to us and reveal what He wants to do. Usually these people are called prophets. Prophets hear the voice of the Lord and speak what God is saying to them. Seers are prophets, but they also have the gift of seeing into the spiritual realm. The prophets and seers are the ones who are called into His counsel. "Surely the Lord GOD does nothing, unless He reveals His secret to His servants the prophets." (Amos 3:7). Who can be a prophet? Paul says in 1 Corinthians 14:5 "I wish you all spoke with tongues, but even more that you prophesied; for he who prophesies *is* greater than he who speaks with tongues, unless indeed he interprets, that the church may receive edification." Speaking in tongues and prophesying are gifts bestowed on man from God through the Holy Spirit which we will go over shortly but the point that I want to make is that God is willing to make us all prophets if our heart is right toward Him and we understand that God wants us to have spiritual gifts for us to draw more people to Him and into a deeper relationship with Him. To be able to do that, we must first be able to "hear" God and know what His council "will and desire" is. It is by us getting close to God that He reveals Himself and His plans to us. God gives us everything we need to bring him glory and he does that in many ways and one of them is through spiritual gifts.

Spiritual Gifts

In 1 Corinthians chapter 12 Paul reveals to us the gifts of the Holy Spirit that are available to us. "Now concerning spiritual *gifts,* brethren, I do not want you to be ignorant: You know that you were Gentiles (non believers), carried away to these dumb idols (other religions), however you were led. Therefore I make known to you that no one speaking by the Spirit of God calls Jesus accursed, and no one can say that Jesus is Lord except by the Holy Spirit. There are diversities of gifts, but the same Spirit. There are differences of ministries, but the same Lord. And there are diversities of activities, but it is the same God who works all in all. But the manifestation of the Spirit is given to each one for the profit *of all:* for to one is given the word of wisdom through the Spirit, to another the word of knowledge through the same Spirit, to another faith by the same Spirit, to another gifts of healings by the same Spirit, to another the working of miracles, to another prophecy, to another discerning of spirits, to another *different* kinds of tongues, to another the interpretation of tongues. But one and the same Spirit works all these things, distributing to each one individually as He wills."

There are some very key points in this passage of scripture that I would like to point out. It says in the scriptures that there are different gifts, different ministries, and different activities, but they are all done through or by God. These are not things that man can do, it is done by God in man and through man. The scripture also goes on to tell why God manifests these gifts, it is to benefit *all*. The scripture also ends with saying that God gives the gifts to each person individually as He wills. That does not mean that God will only want you to have a gift, or some of the gifts, it means that if your heart is right with God and you desire to bring Him glory by living for Him and you earnestly desire the gifts to do that, then you can influence the heart of God to make Him want you to have the gifts. My greatest prayer that I ever prayed was when I found out how much God loves people and I wanted the people to know and realize that God is real and He is a loving and kind Father so I prayer this prayer. "Father I ask you to bestow upon me all the gifts of your Spirit because when this body dies, I will not be able to help anyone or bring you any more Glory in the earth. In Jesus' name" I fully believe that since my heart was to help people and do it for God, and to bring Him glory, it moved Him to answer my prayer and he has bestowed all the gifts upon me and then some. In the manifesting of these gifts, it has made my heart full of joy to see people set free from curses, or give them hope, or completely change their life by a word from God. I worked with a girl and when she walked by me, I heard "8 years old". I thought ok, there's not much I can do with that little bit of information so I just kept my heart on God and my spiritual ears open to him. When she walked by again, I heard in my spirit, "dreadful sorrow". So, I walked up to her and asked her what happened when she was eight years old. Her face was one of shock. She said that her parents had gotten a divorce when she was eight and asked me how I knew something had happened. I explained that as a Christian, I have communication with God through His spirit, and he revealed it to me through a word of knowledge. It was then that the gift of prophecy came over me and revealed to her that when that happened in her life a spirit of dreadful sorrow had come into her and that has caused her to be introverted and depressed but that from this time forward she would never have that again. It was an immediate transformation. She went from being a very quiet and introverted person to being friendly and outgoing and it was as if a new life had sprung up from inside her. The joy that I felt from seeing her set free from the pain of the past was worth setting aside everything and making God number one in my life.

The Call of God

"Arise, shine; For your light has come! And the glory of the LORD is risen upon you. For behold, the darkness shall cover the earth, And deep darkness the people; But the LORD will arise over you, And His glory will be seen upon you." (Isaiah 60:1–2). This scripture is talking about the shekinah glory (the light of Christ) shining through you. That is the white light that people have talked about when seeing visions of the Lord. Moses was called by God to go up into the mountains and he was with God and God gave him the 10 commandments. While being in the presence of God, it made the glory of God shine on Moses' face when he came down from the mountain. (Exodus 34: 29,30) "Now it was so, when Moses came down from Mount Sinai (and the two tablets of the Testimony were in Moses' hand when he came down from the mountain), that Moses did not know that the skin of his face shone while he talked with Him (God). So when Aaron and all the children of Israel saw Moses, behold, the skin of his face shone, and they were afraid to come near him." When you spend time with God, He will make your face shine with His glory. When people look at you, they see God's light. When I spent 5 hours a day in the bible, there were times when people would tell me that I was shining and the presence of God was radiating through me. "The Gentiles shall come to your light, And kings to the brightness of your rising. "Lift up your eyes all around, and see: They all gather together, they come to you; Your sons shall come from afar, And your daughters shall be nursed at *your* side. Then you shall see and become radiant, And your heart shall swell with joy; Because the abundance of the sea shall be turned to you, The wealth of the Gentiles shall come to you." (Isaiah 60:3–5). This is what happens when you spend time with God to where His light shines on you, in you, and through you. So, why should you go and spend all that time with God? Just as it was with Moses, the light of God—the shekinah glory—can shine on you and through you, and the heathen will see it and come. They will repent, and your sons and daughters will come to the Lord instead of being sinful and acting foolish. That's awesome, isn't it? Darkness will also flee at the light of God shining through you and you defeat the devil in whatever way he manifesting.

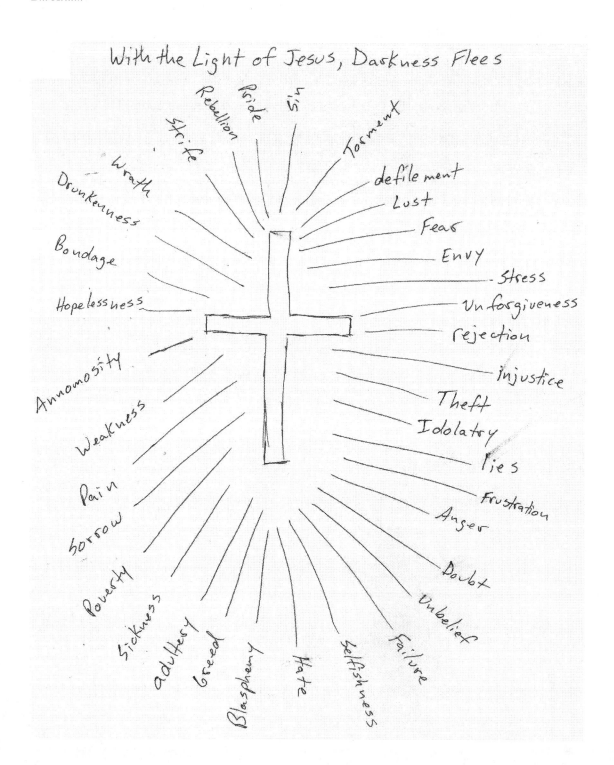

With the Light of Jesus, Darkness Flees

God's Glory through Us

"But we all, with unveiled face, beholding as in a mirror the glory of the Lord, are being transformed into the same image from glory to glory, just as by the Spirit of the Lord."

(2 Corinthians 3:18). Do we hide our face from God and block out His ability to radiate Himself through us because people become uncomfortable when confronted with Holiness? Do we allow the shekinah glory of the Lord to radiate through us? Do we do as Moses did and hide it so that the people don't see the glory of the Lord? We cannot do like Adam and Eve in Genesis 3:7 -10 and hide our faces from the Lord because of sin, for the Lord shows up and says, "Where are you?" God knew where Adam and Eve were! "Then the eyes of both of them were opened (they realized they sinned), and they knew that they *were* naked; and they sewed fig leaves together and made themselves coverings. (tried to cover their sin) And they heard the sound of the LORD God walking in the garden in the cool of the day, and Adam and his wife hid themselves from the presence of the LORD God among the trees of the garden. (Tried to hide themselves) Then the LORD God called to Adam and said to him, "Where *are* you?" So he said, "I heard Your voice in the garden, and I was afraid because I was naked; and I hid myself." When you shine with the glory of God, people will want to hide themselves from you because they will be ashamed because of knowing how sinful they are and fear will grip them but the opposite is what they need to do. We should go to God with our sin and allow Him to cleanse us of it with love and forgiveness and grace. I know the sting of shame and the inner fear of doing wrong and being afraid of being found out. So does God. He knows everything about you, so go to Him anyway. He already knows, but He stills shows up and says, "Where are you?" Why would He show up and call to those who are hiding from Him? It's because He doesn't want you to hide. He says, "I know the secret motives and the roots of why you are the way you are and why you do the things you do. I love you anyway." He wants to change that about you, but you have to go to Him to let Him do it.

Many times He won't change you but will use you just the way you are. It's not about being a perfect vessel but about being a vessel used perfectly. If God can use a donkey (Numbers

61

22:33,34) that has never read His word, meditated on His precepts, or worshipped Him in any way, shape, or form—if God can use that donkey—He can use anything and anybody. Don't allow the sin in your life to come between you and God. Don't allow the Enemy to use guilt and shame to put a hindrance and blockage between you and God having a relationship.

In spite of the shame, Jesus endured the cross. Hebrews 12:2 "looking unto Jesus, the author and finisher of *our* faith, who for the joy that was set before Him endured the cross, despising the shame, and has sat down at the right hand of the throne of God." Jesus did not allow the fear of being ashamed to keep Him from going to the cross for me and you. He wants to help you overcome the sin in your life and be set free from it.

(Psalms 46:1–4). "God *is* our refuge and strength, A very present help in trouble. Therefore we will not fear, Even though the earth be removed, And though the mountains be carried into the midst of the sea; *Though* its waters roar *and* be troubled, *Though* the mountains shake with its swelling. *Selah There is* a river whose streams shall make glad the city of God, The holy *place* of the tabernacle of the Most High." God does this in spite of sin in our lives. He desires us to have peace in our lives by relying and trusting in Him.

Are you the tabernacle (dwelling place) of the Most High? (1 Corinthians 3:16) "Do you not know that you are the temple of God and *that* the Spirit of God dwells in you?".

Psalms 46:5–7 "God *is* in the midst of her, she shall not be moved; God shall help her, just at the break of dawn. The nations raged, the kingdoms were moved; He uttered His voice, the earth melted. The LORD of hosts *is* with us; The God of Jacob *is* our refuge." Has the Lord helped you or done anything for you? Has the Lord done any works in your life? You need to bring to remembrance and set a memorial the things that God has done for you in your life. When you see all the things that God has done for you, you will build your faith in Him that he will continually help you. Take strength and refuge in the promise that "being confident of this very thing, that He who has begun a good work in you will complete *it* until the day of Jesus Christ;" (Philippians 1:6).

God Is for You, Not against You

Jeremiah 29:11 "For I know the thoughts that I think toward you, says the LORD, thoughts of peace and not of evil, to give you a future and a hope." Does that sound like a God that is mean and hates you? When you put your faith in God, he does show that he can bring about some severe punishment but its not toward us. "Come, behold the works of the Lord, Who has made desolations in the earth." (Psalms 46:8). Has anybody ever come against you and became desolated because of it? Has God ever destroyed anybody who has come against you? I have seen it time and time again where God has fought my battles and just had me trust in Him which is sometimes a lot harder that it seems like it should be. We are raised and taught to take care of things ourselves, so trusting in someone else to do something on our behalf is not something that comes natural to us. "He makes wars cease to the end of the earth; He breaks the bow and cuts the spear in two; He burns the chariot (the things that come against us) in the fire." (Psalms 46:9). Concerning the things that come against us, remember that (Isaiah 54:17) "No weapon formed against you shall prosper." Why? Because God breaks the bow, cuts the spear in half, and burns the chariots they came in. God tells us in Psalms 46:10 "Be still, and know that I am God; I will be exalted among the nations, I will be exalted in the earth!" Be still means to be peaceful and quiet on the inside, trusting and relying on the only true, living God. He says to know that He is God. He will be exalted among the nations. He will be exalted in the earth by having whatever comes against you to be defeated for you.

Prophets and Seers

Prophets and seers know God intimately and personally, because they stand in His counsel. They rely solely on the Spirit of God and the help of His kingdom to overcome the earth and the evil in it. They do this by forsaking the devil and the things of this world for the God of everything.

Judging

A lot of prophets have gone out into the world. How do you know the right ones from the wrong ones? Religious spirits get the false prophets to say, "Ah, you shall not judge." We *are* to judge. We are to judge the prophets and their prophecies to expose the counterfeits and separate them from the real ones. 2 Corinthians 11:13–15 says "For such are false apostles, deceitful workers, transforming themselves into apostles of Christ. And no wonder! For Satan himself transforms himself into an angel of light. Therefore it is no great thing if his ministers also transform themselves into ministers of righteousness, whose end will be according to their works." Peter also warns us to judge in 2Peter 2:1-3 "But there were also false prophets among the people, even as there will be false teachers among you, who will secretly bring in destructive heresies, even denying the Lord who bought them, and bring on themselves swift destruction. And many will follow their destructive ways, because of whom the way of truth will be blasphemed. By covetousness they will exploit you with deceptive words; for a long time their judgment has not been idle, and their destruction does not slumber." He tells us to look out for these people and to judge if they are true or false prophets. Beware of those people who are always trying to get you to buy something by telling you that if you give an offering out of love, then "for this week, and this week only—we will give you 10 percent off when you order these tapes." Such people turn the gospel into a business and they tell you to do an offering so that they won't have to pay taxes on what they sell. In my church, we do not take an offering unless there is a specific need for a specific amount. We use no pressure or manipulation, for we have faith that God meets every need. People give out of what they can and the amount needed is met and not a penny more. The church has no funds, no property to maintain, and has no financial burden other than the rent that we pay to have our gathering in the building that we use and people just reach in their pockets and give to the rent. The church keeps none of it. As the pastor of the church, I take no salary or benefits. I do it for God and He blesses me in other ways whether it's through my business or through favor. Our sound system belongs to people in the church and they bring it every week and set it up. The church owns nothing therefore needs no money. "You will know them by their fruits. Do men gather grapes from thornbushes or figs from thistles? Even so, every good tree bears good fruit, but a bad tree bears bad fruit. A good tree cannot bear bad fruit, nor can a bad tree bear good fruit. Every tree that does not bear good fruit is cut down and thrown into the fire. Therefore by their fruits you will know them." (Matthew 7:16–20). We are told to judge between good fruit and bad fruit.

Revelation 19:10 says "And I fell at his feet to worship him. But he said to me, "See that you do not do that! I am your fellow servant, and of your brethren who have the testimony of Jesus. Worship God! For the testimony of Jesus is the spirit of prophecy.". When a prophetic word comes forth, does it glorify God and Jesus Christ? Do they have the testimony of Jesus? What is the testimony of Jesus? What has He done for you? My testimony of Jesus is this: He has completely changed my life, and I didn't do it myself! "Therefore I make known to you that no one speaking by the Spirit of God calls Jesus accursed, and no one can say that Jesus is Lord except by the Holy Spirit." (1 Corinthians 12:3). Do those who claim to be prophets deny the deity or God that is Jesus Christ? John 1:1 proves that Jesus is God. "In the beginning was the Word, and the Word was with God, and the Word *was* God." There are people that call themselves Christians who do not believe that Jesus was in fact God but was just a prophet.

1 John 4:1-6 "Beloved, do not believe every spirit, but test the spirits, whether they are of God; because many false prophets have gone out into the world. By this you know the Spirit of God: Every spirit that confesses that Jesus Christ has come in the flesh is of God, and every spirit that does not confess that[a] Jesus Christ has come in the flesh is not of God. And this is the *spirit* of the Antichrist, which you have heard was coming, and is now already in the world.

You are of God, little children, and have overcome them, because He who is in you is greater than he who is in the world. They are of the world. Therefore they speak *as of the* world, and the world hears them. We are of God. He who knows God hears us; he who is not of God does not hear us. By this we know the spirit of truth and the spirit of error."

Have you ever spoken to people about the things of God, and they look at you like you have just spoken in a foreign language, and they can't grasp the revelation of what you are talking about? Maybe they just call you a nut? God tells us why right there in that scripture. "he who is not of God does not hear us. By this we know the spirit of truth and the spirit of error." The people that do not know God are not spiritually reborn and so they do not understand the things of God and spiritual understanding. Their brain cannot comprehend what you are saying because their brain is only in tune with worldly, natural things and many believe that the bible is a book that some guys just got together and wrote and that it is not the actual word of God. I took a teenager who thought that way and asked him to write down something that I said. After he wrote it, I asked him "who wrote it/" He said that he did. I said, "Ok, who spoke it?" He said, "You did". I explained that is the exact way the bible was made. God spoke it, and the people wrote it down. People wrote it, taking dictation from God as He spoke it. It even says in 2Timothy 3:16 "All Scripture *is* given by inspiration of God," God is speaking scripture to *His* children that are born of spirit. What does God say about His children? He says that "My sheep hear My voice, and I know them, and they follow Me."(John 10:27). This point is also proved in 2Peter 1:21 "for prophecy never came by the will of man, but holy men of God[a]spoke *as they were* moved by the Holy Spirit." The Holy Ghost is not going to reveal scripture and then turn around and come against what the Bible says. False prophets many times speak things that are in contradiction to what God says in His word. Deuteronomy 18:22, "when a prophet speaks in the name of the LORD, if the thing does not happen or come to pass, that *is* the thing which the LORD has not spoken; the prophet has spoken it presumptuously; you shall not be afraid of him." We have seen throughout history that people are running around saying that the world is going to end and all kinds of terrible things are going to happen and in doing so, people act on what they hear even though it doesn't come to pass. Many people in the 1960's build fallout shelters from the threat of nuclear war with Russia. At the turn of the year from 1999 to 2000 (Y2K) everyone was saying that all the computers would crash and the world as we know it would stop. Even in the church there are a lot of people prophesying and teaching to what people want to hear, which is a method of control and manipulation and not teaching and prophesying what God is saying. But for those of us that are born again spiritually, we don't believe in that because we know what God says and we place our faith in that. And since we have the same spirit of faith, according to what is written, "I believed and therefore I spoke, we also believe and therefore speak," (2 Corinthians 4:13) Do the words bear witness with the Holy Spirit in you? They may not, if a spirit that is not of God is speaking to your mind to try and get you to believe a false prophesy or a lie, we can test the spirit behind the words and check God's word (The bible) to see what God has to say about it. And this is where the knowledge of God's word is indispensable.

Sometimes children of God shy away from His words. There is a demon spirit in them that doesn't want them to hear from God or may are fearful of judgement or punishment. I think most of us have felt that way in our own lives when our parents call us and we are apprehensive to go because we don't know if they are calling us to confront us over something we did and so we try and rack out brains to come up with a story and try to figure out "Ok, what did I do that I am in trouble for and what can I say to get out of it !!!." That is a direct representation of Adam and Eve hiding from God in the garden after eating the fruit. (2 Corinthians 3:17) Now the Lord is the Spirit; and where the Spirit of the Lord *is*, there *is* liberty. God already knows everything you will did and will do and you cannot hide anything from Him so when He calls you, don't be afraid. Yes, we will all face judgement but by receiving Jesus' sacrifice for your sins, you are deemed free by His righteousness and not by anything you could ever say or do. So when a word is spoken, does it bring liberty or bondage? As we just read, the Lord brings liberty and the word of God also says that in 2 Timothy 1:7, "For God has not given us a spirit of fear, but of power and of love and of a sound mind." If a word that comes forth brings fear, it is not from the Spirit of God, and it is not a prophecy from God. In Acts 20:30, God also warns us, "Also from among yourselves men will rise up, speaking perverse things, to draw away the disciples after themselves." These are preachers and prophets who want the prestige, power, and want to be the center of attention instead of leading people to God. They preach words to itchy ears much like a politician saying anything to get your vote. "Well, if you come to our church, we preach that you can have all the promises of God, and you can still do this and that." "You don't have to live holy lives." "You don't have to do anything on your part, because salvation is not by works so that men can't boast. This is because God, through Jesus Christ, wants to give everything to you." "The walk of a Christian is an easy walk, because we walk with God. When you walk with God, He takes care of all the world—and even hell when it comes against you. That's why it's easy." People who preach a Christian walk laden with rose petals don't have a clue. There is a devil out there and he does not like you whether you're a Christian or not. John 16:33 tells us "These things I have spoken to you, that in Me you may have peace. In the world you will have tribulation (troubles); but be of good cheer, I have overcome the world." What God is saying is that you are going to have to deal with worldly stuff consisting of bad circumstances that will try to crush our emotions, damage our bodies, and try to get us to lose faith in God but God is saying that through everything, if you remain "in Me" that is, in the spirit of God, you can go through it in peace but to get to that point, you will have to have your faith built by going through things and seeing how God gets you through it so that you can keep focused on Him and not on the thing you are going through. The devil wants to capture your attention and get you focused on what he is doing and off of God's word because he knows that your power to overcome is in God's word.

Seers

All seers are prophets, but not all prophets are seers. It's the understanding of the audible (hearing) and the revelatory (seeing). A prophet hears from God and speaks it forth. A seer sees visions, dreams, and revelations given to him but not necessarily by word, although it *can* be by word, which would make him also a prophet.

I was invited to come to a fellow Christian's house. A guy came from Arizona to meet me for he had heard that I am a prophet and a seer. In the middle of talking to this guy, the Lord showed me an X-ray of the guys wife's midsection that owned the home. There was a black mass type of thing there. I said, "Excuse me just a second." I went over and laid my hands on her and prayed over her quickly, and she began to react to God healing her. Everyone asked me what had happened, but since it was purely of the Holy Ghost, I don't know what He removed. I just went back to talking, and they were kinda like, "What was that, what just happened?" I explained that the Lord showed me a vision and impressed upon me to take care of this, so I took care of it. I don't know what it was. I didn't bother to ask. God revealed it to me in a vision and wanted me to take authority over it and remove it and so I did. God may give you a vision, but He may not necessarily reveal everything about the vision. He may just give you a word of knowledge about the vision. There have been many instances of praying for people and God gives me visions and lets me see spiritually what I am dealing with and sometimes I have to go to Him in prayer and have Him explain the vision to me. You can see Him do the same thing with Daniel and Jerimiah in scripture. God will deposit things in you in a multitude of different ways, whether they are audible, visionary, revelatory, or an unction that is just kind of pushed into your spirit. We must be in a relationship with Him to be able to receive and do the things He wants us to do. God has to develop you to trust Him and overcome everything so that your faith in Him is greater than any fear that may try to come upon you. In doing deliverance and casting out demons there are things that the natural mind of man cannot understand but being spiritually sighted, you understand completely. When you see angels, and demons and the things of the spiritual realm manifested to you in your own eyes as well as in spiritual dreams and visions, the spiritual realm becomes more real to you than the natural realm because you understand that it is the spiritual realm that interjects into the natural and not the other way around. The natural realm never changes the spiritual.

(1 Corinthians 13:13–14:5) "And now abide faith, hope, love, these three; but the greatest of these *is* love. Pursue love, and desire spiritual *gifts,* but especially that you may prophesy. (Why did the Holy Spirit say this if He didn't want us to do it?) For he who speaks in a tongue does not speak to men but to God, for no one understands *him;* however, in the spirit he speaks mysteries. But he who prophesies speaks edification and exhortation and comfort to men. He who speaks in a tongue edifies himself, but he who prophesies edifies the church. I wish you all spoke with tongues, but even more that you prophesied; for he who prophesies *is* greater than he who speaks with tongues, unless indeed he interprets, that the church may receive edification." If you believe that God spoke the bible and man just wrote what God said, then you must also believe that He wants you to prophesy … otherwise He is a nut. The person who prophesies is greater than the person who speaks in tongues unless someone gives interpretation that the congregation can be edified. God is a giver and an encourager, and as His children the prophets and seers we encourage not ourselves but the church. We are the ones who build people's faith and reliance on their heavenly father by revealing what He says to us in words, dreams, and visions.

Man, New Age, and God

I am going to present some differences between New Age spirituality and God. New Age beliefs have stolen the things of God, twisted and perverted them, and caused the children of God to be afraid to walk in them. Christians panic and cry out, "But you can't do that! It is New Age witchcraft!" The devil never created anything new; all he did was steal what God had already done. New Age beliefs concentrate on psychic powers from the spirit of man. God uses His own power with man through a relationship with His Spirit. There is the Spirit of God, the spirit of the Enemy, and the spirit of man. They are all listed in scripture.

The spirit of man has the ability to unleash psychic power into the realm of the spirit to bring about man's own desire. This is where charismatic witchcraft takes the word of God and appropriates it for a person's own glory, prosperity, and desires. New Age enlightens us to what man can do, but God equips us to allow Him to do things through us. Herein lies the difference between New Age and Christianity. In Christianity, God is doing everything with us and for us. In New Age, mankind is doing everything for itself. New Age believes that love is all-accepting. Have you ever seen the bumper sticker that says "Coexist"? The belief behind this slogan says that no matter what people want to do, you have to accept them, because you have to love everybody—as long as you don't try to bring God into it. It is a false love. God Himself is love. Love is His banner, and love comes only from Him through relationship. All others are counterfeit. New Age is worship and idolatry, where man is God and the maker of his own destiny. But when God is in man through a relationship and the indwelling of the Holy Spirit, man walks out the plan of *God* in his life—not his own plan. New Age mindsets in people have minimal power, because their beliefs are based on man. Christians are full of power, because they are based on the Holy Spirit and the word of God. New Age followers think like man, act like man, and have the wisdom of man. Through the Holy Spirit, Christians walk like Jesus, talk like God, prophesy like Jesus, do what Jesus did, and have the wisdom and counsel of God—because the same spirit that is in Him is in His followers. New Age stole the concept of meditation; its followers do it unto their own desires, using psychic powers to obtain what they want. Christians meditate on the word of God and God reveals His desires for us desires.

Psalms 119:13–16 says "With my lips I have declared All the judgments of Your mouth. I have rejoiced in the way of Your testimonies, As *much as* in all riches. I will meditate on Your precepts, And contemplate Your ways. I will delight myself in Your statutes; I will not forget Your word." This is being perfect before God. The devil will try anything to get you to not spend any time thinking about God's word cause he knows that is where your victory over everything comes from. Demons can try to keep you from putting God and His words, statutes, precepts, testimonies, judgments, and ways into your life. They try to do it through mind manipulation, much as the Serpent did to Eve in the garden. God told her not to eat the fruit, but the Serpent said, "That's not what God meant," and he tried to twist Eve's intellect to get her to believe something God didn't say. The Serpent reasoned with Eve and got her to believe that what God had said was not what was going to happen. Serpents captivate the mind and puts its prey into a trance—hypnotizing, swaying, speaking soothing words, and lulling its mind to sleep. He speaks to you and gets you to believe him instead of God. That's why scripture says in Ephesians 5:14 "Awake, you who sleep, Arise from the dead, And Christ will give you light." God was not talking about someone who is actually sleeping; He was talking about those whose minds have been lulled into this dull, trancelike state. The Enemy is like a snake moving back and forth, lulling minds almost into hypnosis. When you hear God, the devil tries to produce a false peace in you, which causes you not to obey God. You become captivated by the fruit. "Look at the fruit," the devil says. "See how beautiful it is. It's going to be tasty and nice to eat." And then the word of God, which says, "Don't touch it," just kind of goes away. When the mind is lulled, it becomes open to suggestion instead of being alert and using reasoning and understanding. The soothing words of the Enemy got Eve to sin. If you do not take every thought captive, the same suggestive thoughts can captivate you.

The Old vs the New

Man and Christ

Before we got together with God, every one of us had a life of walking in sin. Back then, we were in sin and also were among the sinful people of the world. But after you accept Christ and put off the life of sin and put on the life of righteousness by living for God and not your own desires, you have more to change about yourself. Now you also have put off these things "But now you yourselves are to put off all these: anger, wrath, malice, blasphemy, filthy language out of your mouth. Do not lie to one another, since you have put off the old man with his deeds," (Colossians 3:8,9). When we go to get into the realm of God's kingdom, we must remove these things from us. We have (past tense) put on the new man (the man of Psalms 82:6), which is renewed in the *knowledge* (we have to know) according to the image of Him that created us, where there is neither Greek nor Jew (people of different countries), circumcision nor uncircumcision (people of religion), barbarians, Scythians (people of education), bond nor free (people of class structure), but Christ is the only one manifested in the new man. None of these other forms of people exist in Christ. Only Christ exists through them (Colossians 3:10a). Not I who live, but Christ in me (Galatians 2:20). But Christ is all and in all. "Put on, Therefore, as *the* elect of God, holy and beloved, put on tender mercies, kindness, humility, meekness, longsuffering; bearing with one another (put up with each other), and forgiving one another (don't hold any grudges), if anyone has a complaint against another; even as Christ forgave you, so you also *must do*. But above all these things put on love, which is the bond of perfection. And let the peace of God rule in your hearts, to which also you were called in one body; and be thankful. Let the word of Christ dwell in you richly in all wisdom, teaching and admonishing one another in psalms and hymns and spiritual songs, singing with grace in your hearts to the Lord. And whatever you do in word or deed, *do* all in the name of the Lord Jesus, giving thanks to God the Father through Him. (Colossians 3:10–17). God is love, and faith works by love. Not doing these things keep you from walking in love and cause a separation between you and God which is why He says to put these things away from you.

What God Does

There was with the angel a multitude of heavenly hosts praising God and saying, "Glory to God in the highest, and on earth peace, goodwill toward man" (Luke 2:13–14). God laid down His ill will toward men and their sins and chose to have peace with them. He put on love through grace and did away with the sin that divided us and Him and by putting away the sin of all men through Christ. He destroyed the veil of separation between God and man, which was in the temple and separated man from God, so that now we can come boldly, but humbly and full of thanksgiving, before His throne so that He will hear our prayers. He is our God, and we are His people. We strive to forget ourselves that we may know Him.

Regarding our past and our fear of the future, the Lord says, "I AM." When we live in the past with its mistakes, hurts, regrets, and failures, He says, "It is hard because I am not there. My name is not "I WAS." We need to forget those things that are behind us.

When we live in the future, with its anxieties and fears of the unknown, the Lord says, "It is hard. Don't worry about tomorrow, because I am not there. My name is not "I WILL BE."

When we live in this moment, the Lord says, "It is not hard. I am here, for my name is "I AM."

The Enemy uses projections of the future to scare you, and he tries to get you to carry the baggage of the past. Where is the Lord? He is right here. He is with you now. You don't need to suffer the past or worry about the future. Live with God right now. He will take care of all of your needs now and in the future.

God is not a respecter of persons (Acts 10:34). He opened up the heavens for Jacob to see the ladder. (Genesis 28:10-17) He opened the eyes of the prophets to see the angels in the spiritual realm. (2 Kings 6:17-20) He came and visited man and gave His Spirit unto men to have a relationship with them. He did, and still does, mighty miracles in and through men. You are no less and no more than they, and He will do no less and no more for those who call upon the name of the Lord, exercise their faith, and are willing to receive.

As a testimony, I have written here some of the things God has done through people in my own church group that have learned and exercised their faith by hearing the things in this book through my teachings (at the Lord's instruction).

- A woman cast a demon spirit out of her grandson.
- Many people are prophesying and walking in revelations and visions.
- People are getting victory over fear and anger and have allowed God to give grace, peace, and patience.
- People are walking in the counsel of God and listening to the Holy Spirit.
- A woman testified to confronting and binding a spirit in one of her kids. She said, "Put on your seatbelt." He said, "No!" She got right up in his face and said, "I bind that demon in Jesus's name, and you will listen to me and put on that seatbelt." The child responded with "Yes, ma'am" as the response.
- A woman was led by the Spirit to minister to a woman.
- A woman bound the spirits speaking through her mother.
- A man stepped out in faith and confronted a storm, and the storm left.
- The manifestation of the Spirit of God brought healing and deliverance.

Father, allow us to grasp the full revelation of you and your Spirit, and allow us to walk in it, in Jesus's name.

Lots of people say, "I have faith," but what happens when the rubber meets the road? When a storm comes, does their faith collapse and just blow away? Or do they really have faith grounded in the rock of their salvation and say, "Lord, though heaven and earth are moved, I shall only be a witness, because my faith and trust is in You and I command that storm to leave in Jesus' name." That is the person who will stand through the trials and tribulations.

But you have an anointing from the Holy One, and you know all things. (1 John 2:20) This is where you take every thought captive to the obedience of Christ, and you subject the prophetic word to the Holy Ghost, and He will reveal it to you. By subjecting everything to God, you'll know all things. Sometimes God may tell you that you are on a need-to-know basis, and right now you don't need to know, so you take that matter and put it on a shelf. When God deems it necessary for you to know about it, He will reveal it to you. When a five-year-old comes up and asks the parents about the birds and the bees, they say to him, "You know what? You are on a need-to-know basis, and right now you don't need to know." You put that on a shelf and ask him to come back when he's around twelve.

"But the anointing which you have received from Him abides in you, and you do not need that anyone teach you; but as the same anointing teaches you concerning all things, and is true, and is not a lie, and just as it has taught you, you will abide in Him." (1 John 2:27). Take all things to the obedience of Christ, and develop your relationship with the Holy Spirit in order to recognize His voice and know it from the voice of a stranger

Offices of the Ministry

And He Himself gave some *to be* apostles, some prophets, some evangelists, and some pastors and teachers, (Ephesians 4:11). Okay, what are these? These are the offices of ministry. Why does He do this? For the equipping of the saints, for the work of the ministry, for the edifying of the body of Christ. Why? So, we all come to the unity of faith and knowledge of the Son of God to become perfect (Ephesians 4:12). All of these combined provide unity. If a church body doesn't have all of these, the people are not in unity and have not matured into fully perfect men. Man is the bride of Christ (Ephesians 4:13). If you have your arm cut off, are you a fully perfect man? No, you are missing an arm. Scripture says that the first shall be last and the last first. Apostles came first, and then the prophets, evangelists, pastors, and teachers. Let's look at what has happened over the course of time since the fourteenth century after the Dark Ages. The apostles, prophets, evangelists, and pastors were all found in Christ, the perfect man.

Becoming the Perfect Man

In the list found in Ephesians we see the fivefold ministry for the unity and perfecting of the faith and knowledge of Christ the Son, which leads the church into becoming mature and perfect men. What is God doing? He is coming back for His church, "that He might present her to Himself a glorious church, not having spot or wrinkle or any such thing, but that she should be holy and without blemish." (Ephesians 5:27) He is coming back for a perfected man, or a perfected bride, which is Christ perfected in us. And the only way the bride is going to be ready is to be in a state of full maturity and perfection. That is what the scripture says in Ephesians 5:27. Does the church of God right now have unity? No. So, the pure fact that it doesn't have unity means that all of those who are here are not working together. The Bible talks about the first rain and the latter rain. The first rain waters the seed, and the seed comes up and brings forth a little fruit. The latter rain comes before the harvest, and it takes that little fruit and makes it big fruit. The first church was the little fruit. That's why the Bible says that you will do greater things than these. The fruit that is going to be poured out on the children of God in the end times is going to be something the church has not experienced before. God said in Acts 2:17, "And it shall come to pass in the last days, says God, That I will pour out of My Spirit on all flesh; Your sons and your daughters shall prophesy, Your young men shall see visions, Your old men shall dream dreams." There are prophets out there, but the whole church and its prophecy have not matured. Compare the prophets of old with the prophets of today. Do they walk in the same power? Do you see anybody sitting on a mountaintop, calling down fire from heaven and burning up fifty soldiers like Elijah did (2Kings 1:10)? Not yet. Do you see a prophet of God cursing little children, and two bears coming out and ripping them into little pieces (2Kings 2:24)? No. Today's prophets are not walking in the full maturity of that office yet. But they are going to. We have to get the understanding of what God is doing at this dispensation of time. Around the turn of the nineteenth century, Smith Wigglesworth was raising the dead. John G. Lake held a petri dish of bubonic plague, and it died in his hand. These gentlemen did not have a break-in relationship with God; they just flowed in whatever the Holy Spirit wanted them to do. The reason those things are not happening now is that a demonic spirits have come in and caused division between man and God by creating religions. We are all supposed to be in unity with the Holy Spirit. The Holy Spirit is developing your relationship with Jesus Christ, sensitizing you to Him so that if He whispers just a small word, you will be quick to hear it and act on it. He will not contradict Himself, in the Bible or through revelation. The Holy Spirit is not going to say two different things to two different people. He will not have one person preach that it's okay sin, and have another person say that it's not. Until everyone gets in tune with the Holy Spirit, there will be division. The Holy Spirit is not going to contradict Himself. The prophetic word must line up with the word of God. The word of God is the judge of all things. You get some Christians out there who say, "You should not judge. Only God can judge." But God already has. I am just telling you what His judgment is. It is up to you to receive it. Do you want to argue against the word of God? That's on you, and do it away from me, because I don't want to be next to you when your correction comes. The other division comes from people not understanding that we all have things that God has to work out of our lives. Somebody like Peter will become fearful in the flesh. When the Jews came in, Peter left the Gentiles (recounted in the book of Acts) and jumped over to the Jews' side. When someone acts like this, everybody says, "That's not a man of God. He is walking in sin, because he is now a respecter of persons. He is a sinner and is discounting God in His life." They are judging one action—and judging the whole man by that one action. What else does God say He is going to do in these end times? He is going to take the world and shake it, and all these false foundations and religions and man-made control systems will shake apart, because they do not align with God's designs and nothing but God can save people at that time. When the rubber meets the road, and the people in these religions don't have any faith in Christ, when this world starts to shake, what are the people going to do? Look what happened to the people down in New Orleans when hurricane Katrina came through there. Where was the faith of the people? The government didn't save them. The Baptists and Pentecostals didn't save them. You can't put your faith in church or religion. You have to put your faith in Christ and in Him alone. He alone has the power to save you—not your church or government. Be looking for the outpouring of the Spirit of God in these end times, and connect yourself to the Holy Spirit. Relinquish yourself to Him— body, soul, and spirit.God has a plan and a purpose for you. My prayer is that as you have read this book, you will understand that God loves you and wants a relationship with you. He wants you to fulfill the calling He has for your life.

May the favor and blessings of God be upon you always.

About the Author

Bill Arthur started his walk with the Lord in May of 1999. In a very short time, after being born again and baptized in the Holy Spirit, an unquenchable hunger and thirst came over him, and he read the word of God for over five hours a day for a period of about a year and a half. After reading the scripture that says that the Holy Spirit searches the deep things of God (1 Corinthians 2:10), Bill prayed that the Holy Spirit would reveal those deep things to him.

Being led to pray for a healing and deliverance ministry, even before he knew what that was, Bill was led to walk a path where he saw the Lord do many miracles through his hands: healings and demons being cast out through God's word. The gifts and manifestations of the Spirit were on full display, and the Lord gave him revelation through His word of what was happening—and the why and how of it.

Bill has walked in the fivefold ministry as a prophet/seer, teacher, apostle, evangelist, and now a pastor. This is Bill's first book, with many more to follow.

Bill's knowledge of getting people set free from all kinds of bondage, mind-sets, and destructive habits is a revelation given to Bill, but it is for the benefit of the children of the God (Matthew 15:26).